GOOD NEWS IN GALATIANS

in the same series

GOOD NEWS IN GALATIANS

Paul's Letter to the Galatians
in Today's English Version

Introduced by
JOHN D. DAVIES

Collins
FONTANA BOOKS
in co-operation with The Bible Reading Fellowship

First published in Fontana Books 1975

© John D. Davies 1975

Today's English Version of *Paul's Letter to the Galatians*
© American Bible Society, New York, 1966, 1971

Made and printed in Great Britain by
William Collins Sons and Co Ltd Glasgow

*For those in South Africa who are seeking freedom
while under the restriction of banning orders,
particularly for Cos, John, and Steve*

In the midst of death we are in life

CONTENTS

PREFACE

This book is a commentary perhaps. It isn't a technical study on the biblical text, and it isn't based on any original research. But Paul's *Letter to the Galatians* was not a work of research either. It was a response to a very particular ideological situation; in it, he tried to identify *why* people believe what they believe and *why* they commit themselves in the way they commit themselves. In this effort, Paul found that he had to start with himself and explore his own motivations. At the risk of presenting yet another category of theological jargon, I would describe Paul's letter as a piece of motivational theology. In making a sort of commentary on the letter, I have found myself nibbling at a similar kind of exploration.

Of course, the more technically academic studies on the biblical text also derive from a particular cultural and intellectual situation. They depend on certain assumptions concerning analytic method, concerning the nature of scholarly argument, and concerning the manner in which learning takes place. Most of us, in our culture, have absorbed many of these assumptions as we have worked our way through our education system, with its assessment procedures. I am not necessarily rejecting them absolutely; but Paul's assumptions, as a theologian and communicator, were very different. The main reason for this difference is not the arrival of the scientific world-view or any other historical development. The main reason is that Paul was passionately concerned to oppose an immediate and destructive ideological threat, whereas the academic world sets up, as its ideal, the dispassionate concern to add to the store of human knowledge. Paul's work was preaching rather than research; I believe that, if a commentary is at all to reflect the fundamental character of Paul's letter, it will have to be in some way a work of preaching also.

The exposition which follows started life with a very specific purpose in a very specific situation, namely the situation of ideological crisis in South Africa. It is based on some lectures given during Holy Week 1970 at St Paul's College, Grahamstown. At an earlier stage of the development of this book, I included a large number of illustrations of the way in which the *Galatians* situation is mirrored in the conflict between the gospel of Jesus Christ and the ideology of apartheid. But much has been published on this theme in recent years, and South Africans will catch the implications without having them spelled out. I am glad to offer the commentary without those details, because I would not wish to connive in the assumption that there is something uniquely evil about South Africa. Some of us used to get angry with South African government spokesmen for claiming that apartheid was necessary to defend western Christian civilization; now that I have had to be in Britain for a few years, I realize that there is truth in the claim – that apartheid is a development of certain western assumptions concerning human identity, concerning authority, freedom, wealth and success, and that the Christian tradition has been captured and distorted to lend support to these assumptions. So I believe that *Galatians* comes as a fundamental attack not only on apartheid but on many of the assumptions in our wider culture.

Concerning the situation which gave rise to Paul's letter, most of the essential facts can be discovered within the letter itself. I have therefore not supplied a separate introductory essay on questions of this kind; where such information is necessary to the exposition, I have included it at points suggested by the course of Paul's argument, particularly in the first two sections.

The text, including the arrangement and the headings of the sections, is that known as *Good News for Modern Man: the New Testament in Today's English Version* (the TEV). It is a good text. I would, however, advise the reader (unless he can refer directly to the Greek) to check the text against a more literal translation like the Revised Standard Version (Common Bible), because there are points at which the TEV, in my opinion, misrepresents Paul and blunts some of his cutting-edge. Occasionally (e.g. on p. 19) I have supplied a very crude plain translation, in order to emphasize an aspect of Paul's meaning. But these are matters of detail. On the whole, I have learned to value the TEV highly, especially because it is easily the best version in English for people who do not have English as their mother-tongue. Those who speak only English may underestimate the significance of this point; but it does make the TEV a particularly appropriate text for a study of *Galatians*, a document which is much concerned about the problems of communication in a mixed-up cultural setting.

In preparing this commentary, I went back to two great writers on *Galatians*, and I would recommend readers of this book to go back to them also. Go back a century to the Victorian establishment churchman, Bishop J. B. Lightfoot. You will find not only detailed scholarship of great integrity; you will also find a man with a remarkable ability to project himself imaginatively and perceptively into a cultural situation completely different from his own, and to work out a deep social and moral concern that is universal and sometimes deeply moving. Then go back 450 years to the Reformation, when Martin Luther discovered in *Galatians* a precise diagnostic tool for attacking his own situation of ideological conflict; he also found a window into himself to enable his own search for self-awareness, a source of encouragement and healing for the guilt-ridden depressed person whom he calls 'the poor afflicted conscience', and innumerable insights into the spiritual dimensions of political struggle.

I feel that my wife Shirley is as much the writer of this book as I am. She did the typing. She also, in fact, did most of the original perceiving; in doing my own writing, I have often been catching up a few years behind her, and pinning her ideas down on paper.

Lightfoot chose the words 'Why seek ye the living among the dead?' as the motto for his commentary. The claim 'In the midst of death we are in life' would be appropriate for the communities of Christian obedience in South Africa. Actually, however, it is quoted from a community facing similar conflicts and similarly seeking genuine Christian discipleship, in the situation of Ireland. I quote it with great hope for what they are seeking to do and to be.

Pentecost, 1974   JOHN DAVIES

Greeting 1:1–5

1 Paul's first word is 'Paul'. He himself is his point of departure. Before he attempts to say anything else, he speaks of himself. This is not merely a presenting of his credentials; it is a statement of his deepest identity. He is a person who owes his whole character to something which has happened to him, something for which Christian shorthand is 'Easter'.

The *Letter to the Galatians* reveals Paul at his most personal and passionate. He is writing to people who are in serious ideological danger: his letter is an attempt to help them to see the things that are truly most significant about them, and he finds that in doing so he has to explore and state the things that are most significant about himself.

So this is Paul, a man with the political privilege of being a Roman citizen, a man with the religious privilege of Jewish commitment and discipline, a man with the educational privilege of having the ability to use the Greek language to explore an unprecedented kind of personal spiritual history, a man who counts all these special identities as quite insignificant compared with the one new identity which he shares with all members of the Christian brotherhood.

Paul is a true theologian, and *Galatians* is theology at its most valid. Theology is not a range of timeless universal abstractions; it is something which happens, a wrestling with the issues which matter most to people and which motivate them. As an intellectual discipline it requires that the teacher listen to the learner and learn from him, for theology happens in human situations, and the teacher's situation is inevitably several stages away from that of the learner. The theological student needs to be tested not with questions to which the examiner knows the answers but with questions which the examiner has never thought of. The theologian has to be judged not by the evidence that he can give of the books that he has been reading, but by his ability to make creative responses to situations that have never been faced before. Theology is not a concert hall in which ideas are polished and repeated, so much as a laboratory in which critical responses to live situations are made and tested. A truly theological church is always the early church, the first church on a scene where no one has been before. This was how the New Testament books got their form. Anyone who tries to generalize from these books, for instance by writing commentaries, runs a great danger of betraying both the books and the gospel to which they testify. For the gospel of Jesus Christ is about the word becoming flesh, the word becoming history; only too often theology reverses this and replaces history with words. My primary weakness, as a commentator on Paul's letter, is not that I have failed to do my reading, but that I have neither the sensitivity nor the courage really to engage consistently with the historic situation – including the socio-political and economic situation – in which I find myself.

Paul's letter, then, is an attempt to work out a response to a situation which is certainly unprecedented and is also strictly unrepeatable. So he insists that he is not offering a human tradition, a bag of religious groceries. *Galatians* was written for a unique set of conditions; if we would make best use of his writing, we will not attempt to draw morals from it, or distort our perception of our historic situation to fit Paul's situation; but we discover in his response some models for our response to our own situation.

However personal his message may be, Paul has not generated it all from inside himself. He has been sent. He is an apostle, driven by an authority deriving from Jesus, and from God the Father who has enabled this Jesus to be a live person through death. Resurrection is what makes Jesus what Jesus now is: resurrection is also what makes Paul what Paul now is. A major question before Paul's readers is 'what is the deepest truth about us – is it our background, our religious identity, our conditioning, or what?' Paul claims that, while education and conditioning had efficiently made him an agent of human tradition, he is becoming an apostle of Jesus through the raising of the dead.

2 In spite of all the emphasis on his commission and his claim, Paul is no soloist. His greeting is not from himself alone but also from 'the-with-me-all-brothers' (the literal order of his words). A main theme of the letter is the question, 'What is brotherhood?' Are we brothers because we have an ancestry or an identity which most other people do not have? Or are we brothers because of something quite new, something which can be shared with everyone? True brotherhood is Paul's exploration and theme, right to the last verse and the last word of the letter.

Paul addresses his greeting to the churches of Galatia. 'Churches' are not primarily institutions or organizations; they are groups of people in towns and households, who represent certain events to each other. 'Church' is something which happens. 'Church' is a meeting with Easter in people. When Paul writes to 'churches' he is not writing just to identifiable structures; he is writing to people who are *being* church to each other. This remains true, even though his letter is a response to a situation in which they are betraying their character as churches.

Paul writes to 'churches' in the plural. They are scattered and various. They are not a single, monolithic, power-bearing structure. 'Churches', in the sense of alternative styles of church-life, were essential to the solving of the Galatian problem. If that problem had been left to something big enough and authoritative enough to be called '*the* church' (in our modern sense), it is a fair guess that the problem would have been solved wrong: and then there would have been no gospel for us. While the church is limited to an image of its own power, it will tend to tackle only the issues in which there seems a reasonable chance of success; to guarantee itself against failure it will have to protect itself from experiment, and this means it will tend to deal with issues in which it has some confidence in its own competence. It may talk a lot about relevance, but recognize relevance only in things which get through the filtering system which it has itself devised. The church cannot do much to protect itself against all this, because it is a group of

people with human limitations. But it can train its
members to be churches as well as church: it can stimulate and rejoice in the development of *ad hoc* groups
which spring up in response to particular situations,
groups in which issues can be worked out at a local level,
groups which can defy the usual classifications of success
and failure, groups which can be truly experimental,
groups in which church can happen.

The letter is addressed to the churches in Galatia.
Where were these churches? A debate has been going on
for many years among scholars, but there is still no complete agreement. They were towards the north or the
south of the area which is now central Turkey. But the
general character of the Galatian churches is fairly clear.
They were a mixture of several different kinds of people,
drawn together by the preaching of Paul some years
before the letter was written. Some of them had been
converts from Judaism, others were Greek-speaking
Gentiles, others were expatriate slaves, and others may
have been pagan peasants who had not previously been
influenced by the culture of any other group. Some of
them also may have been people whose forebears had
been involved in the Celtic mass-migration from central
Europe a few generations earlier. All of them would be
the subjects of the centralized military bureaucracy of the
Roman Empire. So, whatever else may be true of these
people, they were a very mixed crowd, experiencing all
sorts of insecurity and rootlessness in culture and politics.
In this respect they were like many other groups among
whom the church has grown in times of large-scale
movements of population.

3 Paul often uses this greeting of 'grace and peace'; it is
particularly appropriate to *Galatians*, which is one of his
earliest letters. The Galatians were in two dangers: first,
the danger of thinking that sectional identities of culture,
religion and behaviour are all-important to human
security: second, the danger of thinking that people of
different groups are necessarily hostile to each other and
that we can save ourselves by asserting our differences
and keeping apart. The response to the first danger is the
grace that is from God the Father and from Jesus Christ:

the response to the second is the peace that is from God the Father and from Jesus Christ.

4 It is an evil situation in which we find ourselves, and the will of our God and Father is to liberate us from this. Paul is not just speaking of a spiritual general deliverance in an 'other world': he is primarily thinking of God's purpose to liberate the Christian community from the kind of social and ideological evil which has enslaved the Galatians' minds and which is preventing them from experiencing grace and peace. This is the specific manifestation of the present age of evil which is showing itself: the apostolic witness has to attack specifically if it is to represent the gospel of Jesus. The gospel is about things happening to people in particular historical situations: it is not just the filtering through of timeless ideas from a remote world where there are no real people. If one cannot tell the period and context in which a theologian is writing, the chances are that he is not truly a theologian at all. And, even in Paul's experience, the theological laboratory of Galatia is quite different from that of Colossae or Rome, and the gospel which is drawn out of that situation is unique and specific.

5 Paul ends his greeting with an exclamation. 'To God be the glory.' There is no theology without praise. Orthodoxy is not just right belief but right worship. Christian truth is betrayed when theology is understood as a way of thinking and talking, divorced from acting and worshipping. The Christian gospel is based in event and story rather than argument; its fundamental design is aimed at our imagination and our intuitions as well as our intellect.

The discipline of genuine worship is the deepest way in which we are trained in valuing the purposes and intentions of God. True worship is an announcement to all the tyrants that against them stands a critic and a victor. It is an announcement that opposition to false gods and false gospels is valid and worthwhile. And if I associate myself with this announcement, if I sing it, I am celebrating this victory of the true authority and rejoicing in his critique. True worship is not an anaesthetic, a frivolous diversion of energy from the battles for justice and righteousness. To give glory to the one God of all people, when all around us are demagogues and tyrants and traditions and ideologies demanding our supreme commitment, is a deep political defiance. Theology should not be assessed only in terms of its intellectual neatness, or by its conformity to a historic tradition. Christian theology, from the first, has really been judged by its power to nerve the human spirit to face the tyrannies, the principalities and powers that threaten to obstruct the kingdom of God and his righteousness. Only too often, good initiatives in the battle run out of steam and end in discouragement, not because the basic ideas were wrong but because of inadequate motivation. It is precisely in this area that both theology and worship have a strategic place. Far from being an anaesthetic, worship should be the most powerful political stimulant of all.

The One Gospel 1: 6–10

6–9 But the God whom Paul worships is the God whom the Galatians are deserting. This desertion is rapidly infectious; the lie spreads fast. It is not just a matter of a mistaken opinion; Paul accuses them of disowning the most important thing about them, the grace of God. This is always the fundamental question to be put against any church or Christian tradition: is it really enabling people to live by grace, the surprising unpredictable gift of God for all the world, or is it trapping people in a narrower identity of some cultural group? When a church does disown the grace of God, part of the gospel is that God still has a means to express his judgement. The indignant apostle represents the adaptable strategies of God's persistent love.

Before going further, let us try to identify the problem more specifically. We can discover the essential facts from the letter itself. From the midst of the variegated membership of the Galatian churches, it appears that a group of people had emerged who started to unsettle the minds of the rest. These people were in the churches founded in Galatia by Paul; they had at first been satisfied with the gospel of Jesus Christ as Paul had preached it. But at the crisis-point which forced Paul to write, they had come to the conviction that this gospel was inadequate. They had sought to make up for this inadequacy by turning to the Jewish tradition and accepting at least part of the disciplines of the Jewish law. In particular, they had sought to acquire circumcision, the insignia of Jewish identity. They felt that Paul had short-sold them and overpersuaded them, that he was no more reliable than any other agent of religious ideas and human traditions. They alleged that he had been a spokesman instructed by the churches in Jerusalem and Judea, that he had once himself advocated circumcision but had later omitted this part of his preaching so as to make an easier appeal to Gentiles; that he had been offering the gospel in an incomplete form, and had been recalled by Jerusalem to receive further instructions – these are allegations which Paul denies at various points in his letter. In short, these people felt insecure with the gospel which they had received, and felt a need to supplement it with obedience to the law. The crucial identifying point is that they were people who 'are being circumcised' in the present. This seems to imply that they were not Jews, who would have been circumcised in infancy, but dissatisfied Gentile converts. (For detailed argument on this point, see J. Munck, *Paul and the Salvation of Mankind* [SCM Press, London, 1959], pp. 87–90, and the whole of Chapter 4. For a different view, see F. F. Bruce's series, *Galatian Problems*, in the Bulletin of the John Rylands Library, Manchester, especially Vol. 53, No. 2, Spring 1971.)

If this is so, Paul's problem with the Galatian churches can be seen as a typical specimen of a great many problems that have beset the church from that day to this. It is from people like this that trouble has frequently come, people who find it difficult to live with true Christianity's carelessness about externals, and who feel insufficiently supported by the apparently vague qualifications of the Christian apostolate. Such people look enviously at the strong identities displayed by other groups, such as the Jews. They feel that the inclusive fellowship of the gospel leaves them with too few recognizable characteristics, and so they seek for things to do which will mark them as either 'in' or 'out'.

The problem, therefore, is not caused by Jews. Jewish Christianity is not more sinister than any other national expression of Christianity. Paul is not attacking those Christians who remain Jews. He is defending the right of non-Jewish Christians to remain non-Jewish. Jewish Christianity was a precious growth which unfortunately never became really strong. But we who are Gentiles would have betrayed something more precious if we had fulfilled the demand that we must first become Jewish. There is no special uniform Christian language or cultural style. When people come to feel that the language or accent derived from their parents is unsuitable for God, they are victims of one of the most grievous forms of corporate cruelty; if they yield to this pressure, it is not a demonstration of the power of God but of the ability of a cultural imperialism to use religion as part of its armament. Indeed, one important detail of the Pentecost story is that, although all the crowd were Jews, they were members of all sorts of national groups, and they heard the wonderful works of God proclaimed in their own native languages, and not just in the powerful languages of religion, culture and government (see Acts 2:8–11). Speakers of minority languages have a voice and a song for God; they don't have to be ventriloquized by the powerful in order to be accounted holy.

Christ is the new authority coming to claim all our cultures. Certainly there may be elements in our cultures which are incompatible with obedience to him. But Christ is the new power on the scene; in due course Christ as fulfiller will show what he can claim and Christ as critic will show what he must displace. The co-existence of Christ and his antecedents, which is called syncretism, is confusing and delaying; but it is not fundamentally dangerous.

The real danger, far more serious, is this Galatian aberration, which is usually called 'Judaizing'. Here, Christ is not the new but the old, and Christian members feel that he is not enough. Judaizing is not a throwback or a survival, but an attractive novelty. It happens when people who are already Christians look for a stronger form of religion, with plenty of insignia, which gives clear means for distinguishing those who are 'in' from those who are 'out'. Jewish law is only the first of many different identities which have been employed to serve this demand. Whatever the form, the result is a strong, dynamic and infectious cancer of racial religion.

We may find the whole argument of *Galatians* in one preposition in verse 8. 'If we, or an angel from heaven, should evangelize *besides* what we have evangelized to you.' If anyone should try to add to the gospel which I have given to you, a curse on him. There is all the difference in the world between adding Christ to something and adding something to Christ. Judaizing is the cleverest ideological enemy of the gospel; it inevitably works inside the Christian community: it can attack anywhere and spread its infection by any means. None of us can assume that we are immune to it. This is why *Galatians* is always a contemporary document.

Paul treats this deviation to a false gospel as a critical emergency. What the Galatians are turning towards has all the features of a gospel. He accuses them of turning to another gospel which is not another gospel. To sharpen the distinction a bit more clearly, he accuses them of turning to an additional gospel which cannot be an alternative gospel. The error to which they are turning is a gospel and isn't a gospel. It is a gospel because it is perceived as good news; it isn't a gospel because it leads away from the real truth. It is a counter-gospel, and so is incompatible with the true gospel.

This sort of thing does not happen by accident. General terms are too vague. These things happen because particular people do them. Paul has no hesitation in saying that there are people around who are trying to reverse the gospel of Christ. It is part of the work of the apostle to indicate these people, to expose their purposes and methods. Paul's anger and alarm and curse are not stimulated by a mere mistake in teaching or by a faulty specimen of behaviour. The disorder which calls up this response is one where the very heart of the gospel of Jesus Christ is being denied, not just in words but in fellowship. In terms of the Galatian situation, it is clear that the really basic question is not faced in terms like 'Do you believe in God?' or even 'Why did Christ die?'

The story in chapter 2 shows that the basic question was, 'Who are you willing to eat with?'

Paul had discovered that Christian conversion is not just a series of new things to say, or even new things to do, but a completely new way of relating to other people. For this reason, a situation which forbids people to eat together is far more dangerous than one which disseminates faulty doctrine. The gospel which Paul preached is more than a series of valid propositions concerning Jesus; it is a commendation and explanation of a revolutionary social experience of which Jesus is the origin, cause, agent and fulfilment.

Paul does not curse casually. His curse is a sign of his seriousness, not of his frivolity. It was not the advancement of science that dethroned theology, so much as the advancement of middle-class good manners. Cursing has become defused. But to be accursed is the same as to be outcast. Communication is broken. There are times when such a course of action can *communicate* (in the sense of getting something through to another person's mind) far more effectively than through the usual channels. Diplomacy can make us believe that things are all right so long as the diplomatic people go on talking. But sometimes the curse, the ending of diplomacy, can speak more clearly.

10 Paul is ruthless and insistent with his curse. He is aware that he will alienate some people, especially those with whom he is culturally most closely identified. In such a situation, all the pressures are against breaking ties with one's kith and kin and against maintaining ties with people of other origins.

Paul is not primarily concerned to secure a majority for his point of view; at one time, he suggests, he might have been accused of being conciliatory, but now it must be clear to everyone where he stands, without any compromise. At this point, the procedures of democracy are no guarantee of righteousness; the pursuit of a majority vote would be incompatible with obedience to Christ. Paul represents, at this point, Christ the bringer of crisis rather than Christ the bringer of peace. The irony is that he has been accused of adjusting his teaching to be attractive to people; he has been accused of lowering standards to get cheap support. The same teaching which drew these accusations now causes him to be unpopular. His teaching has not changed: but in some situations it is attractive, in some it is repulsive. Sometimes good Christian witness does happen to be attractive and numerically successful; but sooner or later something will happen to sort out the people who really value the genuine Christ and those who value only the image of success and security. At this point the church has to insist on maintaining its commitment to Christ even when this brings accusations of disloyalty. A church which is in a success-situation should consciously educate its members in the disciplines of creative failure. This will almost certainly mean taking them away sometimes from the visible symbols and structures of ecclesiastical strength, and giving them some live experience of loneliness.

How Paul Became an Apostle 1:11–24

11–14 Paul now describes how the gospel has worked out in his own history. He insists that his commitment to the gospel was not brought about by the success of anyone's influence on him. This is rather discouraging. After all, we reckon that personal influence is usually the biggest factor in the process of conversion. It is, indeed, a principle of the incarnation and of the church that God does not work at people individually by means of a kind of direct spiritual ray; he works characteristically by means of the hit-and-miss system of personal contact. God's primary means of grace is people. But Paul's argument here is a very rare one; if this claim of direct revelation were the most important fact about the gospel, we would surely find him using it as a universal guarantee, as the clinching argument at every point. In fact, this claim is dragged out of him by the peculiar circumstances and challenges which he is facing at this juncture. His whole argument here is that he is stooge or spokesman or dummy for no one; he has not even had his teaching vetted by the church authorities in Judea. The Galatians can accept that he is not an agent of someone's plots;

they need not suspect that any pressure has been brought
to bear on him to water down the gospel, or to offer anything other than the truth as he has been convinced of it.
Our activities cannot be free if we are doing them in
order to fit in to someone else's programme, like a tourist
who can see only what the guide-book tells him to see.
As a man who has himself experienced liberation, Paul
is insisting on taking responsibility for his own decisions.

Unless the gospel is a revelation, it is not a gospel.
When a person really hears the gospel, and is captured
by it, he may well start looking somewhat unbalanced
and absurd, like a person who has just fallen in love.
He may well talk as if everything is happening for the
first time. Indeed, because he is a unique individual,
what is happening to him *has* never happened before;
and the direct contact with Christ may well make the
mediating human agencies seem very unimportant. A
church which allows itself to be ruled by its fear of the
unexpected, of the unbalanced and absurd, may well
find that it is in fact a conspiracy against the gospel of
Christ; and, by the same process, it is likely at the same
time to be a conspiracy against human love and surprise.

15–24 But Paul is not suggesting that God had acted
precipitately. On the contrary, the revelation was the
point where he became conscious of what had been true
about him all along. He had been chosen from before
birth to be an agent of the gospel of Jesus Christ. Further,
his birth had not been caused only by a force that pushed
him *out from* the womb; it had been in some way due
to a power that called him *into* the outer world. His
destiny had come to be a stronger influence than his
origin.

Both in verse 16 and verse 24, Paul uses this rather
puzzling expression 'in me'. 'God revealed his Son in me.'
'They glorified God in me.' Most modern translations
(including the TEV) offer apparently simpler versions of
these phrases, but they all miss some of the full meaning
represented only by the literal translation. The revealing
of God's Son '*in* me' means at least this: that I am not
only the receiver of revelation, but other people receive
revelation because of what has been revealed to me; also,

that I am not only an intermediary for the benefit of others, but the whole process is making a profound difference to myself: and that the Christ who is revealed is not a new arrival; he has been 'in me' all along, but this fact is only now being disclosed. Paul does not speak of his 'conversion'; he is less conscious of having been changed than of having shown the truth about himself.

This event in the depths of Paul's being was not just for his own benefit but in order that he might be an agent of Christ to the Gentiles. He believed himself to be chosen by God. Unfortunately, this doctrine of God's 'election' is taken by many people to mean the selecting of a minority group for special prestige, over the rest of mankind. It has appealed to people's desire to be distinctive, and has been tragically misappropriated by the propagators of apartheid. There is no part of Christian teaching and symbolism which can be more dangerously perverted to serve sectional interests. But the doctrine of election is a vital part of the human attempt to express God's plan both for the church and for the individual. It is, for instance, a fine and precious thing to be convinced that 'God loves me.' But it is a more specific, dynamic, and in some ways more alarming thing to be convinced that 'God chooses me.' God is both the universal lover and the particular chooser. A church which represents his gospel will generate both a welcoming openness and a cherishing closeness.

Paul is chosen as a person in whom the Son of God is to be revealed: he is chosen both to receive the truth and to enable other people to see truth. He is chosen to be a means whereby the Gentiles may know their real security. Paul's chosenness does not make other people subservient to him; on the contrary, it makes him their servant. But even this distinction is a temporary one, because he is chosen to be the means by which these others may come to know their own chosenness. So the effect both of Paul's autonomy and of Paul's chosenness is not to provide a new prestige or master-role for Paul. Paul's liberation is God's success in him: those who perceived it, he says, 'glorified, in me, God'.

Paul and the Other Apostles 2: 1–10

1–2 For fourteen years the churches established by Paul lived a distinct life. They were not part of any external ecclesiastical empire; they had an authentic separate development. But this was not a development of separateness for the sake of separateness; it was a temporary phase, and it ended when Paul became convinced that they ought to move towards a more conscious brotherhood with the Jerusalem establishment. This was not just a matter of expediency or reasoning; nor was it a matter of ecclesiastical obedience. It was due to a revelation, an event of the same order as his conversion. It is an act of God when a man like Paul realizes that such a clear change of policy is needed.

The initiative to bring frontier-church and establishment-church together came, typically, from the frontier-church. The frontier-church is a church that is still very much *becoming*: the establishment-church is a church which already *is*. The becoming group is less obvious and demonstrable than the existing group, and is likely to be reckoned more expendable. The members of the existing group are seen as persons, while the others are seen as statistics or as problems: their status is second class. Even in churches which are theoretically integrated, there are few people who are able to make bridges between these two groups. And where this difference of group-style is further identified with a difference of race, the church can quickly find itself trapped in a structure that merely affirms human divisiveness and does nothing to heal it.

This kind of problem would be familiar to Paul. He was concerned to develop not merely a Gentile church but Gentile maturity and confidence. Christians in his day must sometimes have had the feeling that, in the last resort, a Jewish Christian was worth more than a Gentile one. A Jew was likely to be more reliable; he had a better background; one could be more sure that he had joined the church with intelligent and pure motives, and so on. No one could call a Jew a heathen. This sense of the value of the Jew may well have been paradoxically strengthened by the Jew's lack of political status. His very character as a second-class person in the Roman Empire would drive him to assert this first-class value as a man of religion. Paul, the religious Jew of Tarsus, who was also a Roman citizen, had peculiar advantages for seeing both the value and the limitations of these various identities.

Another worthwhile fact to notice in this procedure of Paul is that he took the initiative to build bridges before any crisis blew up. He knew enough about Jewish sensitivities to realize that his mission to the Gentiles would sometime have to be explained. But he made the essential distinction between letting other people's sensitivities affect one's movements and letting them affect one's policy. The easy procedure is to shape one's policy in the light of possible criticism and then to keep quiet: the bolder course is to shape one's policy according to conscience and then move across to the possible critics and present them with it. Paul went all the way to Jerusalem to tell the institutional leaders what he had been doing, to share with them the gospel which he was convinced was the true gospel in his situation – and 'gospel' at this point must mean not only the propositional content but the whole approach and policy by which the gospel is conveyed. He went to Jerusalem not to tell the authorities what he had been doing (so that his results could be assessed) nor to tell them what he hoped to do (so that his programme could be approved). He went to tell them what he was actually doing. His purpose was not to gain support but to dispel ignorance. The great mistakes which are made by administrative headquarters, which are often so obvious to the humbler workers in the field, are not always due to stupidity, cowardice or fear of change: they are often due to the fact that people at the centre know only what they are allowed to know.

3–5 Circumcision now appears in the story. Later in the letter, Paul deals with circumcision in the broadest theoretical terms. But the first mention of this matter is in connection with a quite specific episode, one which typifies the general issues involved. Paul took Titus to Jerusalem and did not yield to the pressure for him to be

circumcised. To have given way to this diplomatic suggestion would have undermined his witness and set a
false precedent. At this point, compromise would have
been a false move. But this is not because circumcision
is the arch-enemy; in itself, circumcision is not important
enough to obstruct Christ's salvation. What does obstruct
salvation, what does distort human identity and maintain
separation, is the use of external things like circumcision
as the essential insignia of acceptability. Paul rejected the
use of the circumcision of Titus as a bargaining counter.
A person who treats circumcision like that is seeing only
a foreskin and not a person, and this is a way of denying
Christ in that person.

In a situation where external features of men are
given power to decide, literally, matters of life and of
death, of love and fellowship, of mutual care and common worship, the most powerful symbols and motivations available to man are needed to break down the
underlying attitudes of disorder. Generalized sentiments
about love and human value do not get deep enough into
our imagination to have the necessary power. But in
spite of all the misrepresentation and compromise in
Christian history, Christ had this power. This Christ
faces us not only with what we ought to do; this Christ
also goes to the heart of our nature, to the deepest
springs of motivation and personal identity. And all this
was focused hundreds of years ago in the question of
whether a certain Titus should undergo one of the most
trivial forms of surgery.

Paul was not prepared to be deflected from the true
path by the presence of spies or informers. Such people
create embarrassment and anxiety, because they usually
succeed in concealing their identity and thus build up a
general atmosphere of suspicion around them. Paul's
policy is to ignore them, to refuse to accept that they
are a danger, to refuse to allow them the miserable and
destructive identity of spy. At least, this means that they
will be given true facts to transmit; such spies often
succeed in gumming up their own communications-
systems by trying to transmit a whole lot of accurate
statements which they cannot understand or evaluate.

6–9 So six men met. Paul, accompanied by the uncircumcised Greek Titus and the thoroughly Hebrew Barnabas, came to meet James, Peter and John, the leaders of the Jerusalem church. It is impossible to exaggerate the importance of this meeting, the first and probably the only meeting of the four key members of the church's apostolic foundation. The decisions of such a meeting would carry such weight as to be almost impossible to reverse. If these four men had come to a different conclusion, it is safe to say that no church could have survived for long afterwards. Not only would the community have collapsed, but there would have been no one left with any incentive to treasure and record the traditions concerning Jesus' activities and teaching. This has to be borne in mind by people who accuse the early church, and especially Paul, of distorting the original gospel of Jesus. If anything remained to this day it would be merely an archaeological relic, like the Dead Sea scrolls, with no community around it.

At the meeting, there were present those people who 'seemed to be something'. They were people of reputation, the recognized leaders. Paul is certainly not trying to say that their leadership was *only* apparent, that it was fraudulent: if their leadership was invalid in this sense, he certainly would not record the agreement and shake hands with them. What he is emphasizing is that these men's leadership was not a matter of an ineradicable mystical status which fundamentally altered their humanity. Their leadership was a function, which was willingly acknowledged and consented to. It would have been little use for Paul to have spent a great deal of energy on reducing the importance of the distinction between Jew and Gentile, if he had compensated for this by setting up a new kind of magical distinction of status between the apostolic hierarchy and the rest of the disciple community.

These leaders had nothing to add to Paul's gospel. They found nothing missing in it. They acknowledged that Paul's gospel was complete without any insistence on circumcision, the one element which Paul's enemies would expect the Jerusalem church to insist on. In other words, Jerusalem agreed that the community of Jesus Christ was to be a community without insignia. It is impossible to exaggerate the importance of this agreement. It meant that a totally new kind of way of being a person had been inaugurated – not by the conference, which was only recognizing established facts – but by the creative act of God in Jesus Christ. Whereas other people, including Jews, can state quite properly the qualifications for membership of their community, the Christian can never be too sure. He can never say quite absolutely what being a 'Christian' means, or indeed whether it is important to be a 'Christian' at all. Christians are a uniquely ignorant people; more than anyone else in the world, they do not know the answer to the simple question, 'How do we recognize each other?' The mere existence of a community of people who are responsibly careless about this question should be enough to disturb the world's whole style of being.

James, Peter and John recognized that Paul's ministry was every bit as valid and important as Peter's. They recognized that in Paul's work the same basic things had been happening as had been happening in Peter's work, only that Peter had been 'energized' by God towards the Jews and Paul towards the Gentiles. They recognized that, while there is one gospel, there are also specialized ministries. They were convinced that Paul was truly an agent of the grace of God; so they, the recognized pillars of the church, welcomed Paul and Barnabas as fellow-workers, giving them pledges of their confidence.

10 Before the meeting ended, the suggestion was made that Paul and his associates should 'remember the poor'. This may have been a request, a recommendation, or an agreement; Paul does not say. In fact, he records the matter in a sentence which has no main verb at all. We could translate his words: 'The only other matter raised was that we should remember the poor: I myself was very keen to do exactly this.' This is a very unemphatic way of recording the extra item on the agenda. The conference was not suggesting that Gentile Christians ought to pay money to the 'poor' (i.e. the Jerusalem church) to buy their right to be considered proper Christians. The decision is one sign of the work of the Holy Spirit who, from Pentecost onwards, has shown his influence by making people face the call to share in some sort of community of goods.

Paul Rebukes Peter at Antioch 2:11–14

11–12 In Jerusalem, James and Peter and John were remote from the practical implications of the issue of the Gentile mission; a lot of Paul's problems must have seemed to them to be theoretical, if not slightly fanciful. But when he visited Antioch, Peter faced the problem in real life. At Antioch, a much more cosmopolitan city, there was a mixed church, with a significant proportion of non-Jews. At first, Peter was prepared to forget his Jewish identity and to eat with these people. But then some men came from James, from Jerusalem, and Peter withdrew from the table, and his place was empty. He was afraid of 'those from the circumcision'. This is the literal translation. Paul is not identifying them as people who wanted definitely to inflict circumcision on Gentiles, as the TEV translation suggests; they were simply people who were characterized in terms of the fact that they had been circumcised.

With their arrival, Peter's behaviour ceased to be just a private matter; it became observed; it could lead to people being offended, shocked, and discouraged from going any further with their Christian membership. Peter realized that there were consciences other than his own to be concerned about. He discovered how quickly one reaches the boundaries of so-called 'private morality'. If you are Peter, you are conspicuous, whether you like it or not. In such a situation, the need to protect the sensitivities of the people whom we know gets priority over the need to stand up for our fellowship with the people whom we don't know. The under-privileged man will rightly judge the privileged man by watching for the point at which the rights of the under-privileged become expendable. If the pastor chooses to act as guardian and protector of the sensitive members of his own national group, he may well be doing them the greatest possible harm; and he also will be demonstrating that when it comes down to real live issues, the community of race is more important than the community of grace.

But freedom of relationship cannot be established by legislation. Legislation can permit freedom, it can release people for freedom; it can knock down fences; but it cannot force people to love each other in practice. No law could be enforced that could prevent Peter from his sin at Antioch. To attempt to make such a law would bring the church back into the whole legalistic system which still had Peter partly in bondage. Peter has to see simply that some attitudes and actions are incompatible with the gospel of Jesus Christ. These things are not *facts*, learned once for all; and a church which teaches ethical and relational attitudes as if they were obvious, universal, objective matters of fact may be strangely disappointed when this teaching is tested by real hard situations.

The occasion of the trouble at Antioch was not a theory but an activity, the very universal and secular activity of eating. It is typical of the religion of the Bible that the real crisis should take place not at the conference table but at the dinner table. The first conflict in church history of which we have direct evidence – for *Galatians* is one of the earliest parts of the New Testament to be written – was not about words or formulae but about who could eat with whom. That is not to say that it was not a theological conflict. It was theological through and through. Peter's action was a specimen of heretical behaviour, and Paul responded to it in theological terms, in terms of the gospel of the cross of Christ. It is never sufficient merely to get the creed and the liturgy right. Christianity is a matter of making the necessary connections. Often we may make the connections wrong and get things out of proportion. But a church which wanted relics of its really great moments would not look for bones and hair in Jerusalem; it would look in Antioch for a chair which Peter failed to sit in, and for a piece of bread which he did not eat.

13 Peter's sensitiveness about 'what other people will think' was perfectly justified. He was so concerned about his possible enemies that he led into scandalous danger his real friends. The other Jewish Christians resident in Antioch were affected by his 'hypocrisy', by his assumption of a false role: the word used does not refer to a person's motivation but to the false impression which his behaviour produces. A course of action based on fear will usually have more appeal than one based on confidence; particularly this is true when the fear is a fear of repudiation by old friends and the confidence is confidence in the security of one's association with new friends. The effect of Peter's action was that this hypocrisy became a flood, catching up all the Jewish Christians, including Barnabas, *even* Barnabas. Barnabas is one of the most attractive and encouraging characters in the Bible. Barnabas is the kind of man who can make a man like Paul tolerable. Only a man of unusual resilience would care to have Paul as a friend. In an emergency, however, the awkward person may well be right and the nice person wrong. A Barnabas on his own would realize only too late that he has been more obedient to the image of his own goodness than he has been to the calling of Christ.

14 Paul saw that Peter and Barnabas were wrong. They were wrong not in telling lies, or in breaking laws, but in failing to *walk* on the path that goes towards the truth of the gospel. It is a sign of theological weakness that we do not have an English word which adequately translates Paul's term here. We have separated 'theology' from 'ethics'. We have produced the word 'orthodoxy', meaning the right way of expressing Christian truth in statement and worship; but we have not derived a similar word 'orthopody' from this word of Paul, a word which seems to be his own invention. 'Orthopody' would mean the whole complex of commitment, attitude, motivation and behaviour which is based in the gospel of Jesus Christ. And we might use the term 'orthopod' to describe a person who walks according to the truth of the gospel.

Paul identifies the action of Peter and the rest as a basic subversion of the gospel. To withdraw from fellowship on grounds of a difference of race and culture is to forsake Christian tradition: it is a disgraceful innovation, and Paul is reacting as a conservative when he is shocked to see it.

Now, if all that Peter had done was just a violation of usual moral standards, like putting a hatchet through Barnabas's skull, the matter could have been dealt with by a private rebuke. But Peter's refusal to eat with a Gentile was a different kind of crime altogether. It was a public repudiation of the gospel by a conspicuous person. A quiet word of correction in the corridor outside might have convinced Peter, but it would not have rectified the damage done in the community. So Paul spoke to Peter in the presence of the whole membership. Where a significant attack has been made on the gospel in public, and especially where this has been done by a prominent and respected member, the rejoinder must be made in public too; and some people will have to learn that the church cannot always be kept quiet and uncontroversial.

But we should notice the people and groups whom Paul did not attack. He did not attack James, the leader of the Jewish Christians in Jerusalem, nor did he attack the Jewish Christians who continued as Jews in a Jewish area respecting the Jewish law and tradition. He did not attack the institution of circumcision itself. He might have had a much clearer argument if he had felt able to attack in this way.

Even Paul's response to Peter was not an attack on Peter as a person; it was a very specific question about Peter's behaviour; it drew out the implications of Peter's action in withdrawing from the common table. It was not an absolute condemnation; it was, in fact, a commendation of Peter's general way of life, and an appeal to him to be consistent and realize the effects of his actions. It could be offered as a model of Christian critique. Paul was not attempting to undermine Peter's personal value; he was directing attention to what Peter's behaviour looked like, the way that it was received by other people. This is the only way in which Paul's question makes sense. He asked, 'How can you oblige Gentiles to adopt Jewish customs?' Peter could reasonably have answered that he was doing no such thing, that he was only trying to retain the confidence of the people from Jerusalem. 'But,' Paul insists, 'your action of withdrawal is going to be seen by Gentiles as a warning that they cannot expect reliable fellowship with you unless they adopt Jewish customs and so cease to cause awkward situations.'

Peter's action would have been tolerable and intelligible if he had, in his own personal life, been sticking rigidly to Jewish custom: but he had already yielded to the practice of living as a Gentile, so his withdrawal was a threat and a puzzle to people who did not have his advantages, in respect of choice of behaviour. This again is a specimen of a much wider problem, that the man of the 'superior' culture may tantalize the less privileged person by the sheer flexibility by which he can change his behaviour from day to day and from circumstance to circumstance.

Jews and Gentiles Are Saved by Faith 2:15–21

15–21 This section is crucial to the whole letter, for it is here that Paul develops the deepest account of the conflict between the gospel of Jesus Christ and any ideology of legalism or racialism.

'Yes,' he says, 'there are real privileges for those who belong to Jewish culture: we do have moral standards, and in comparison to us there really is a valid sense in which Gentiles can be called "sinners". But because of this very fact we know better than anyone that the endless battle to make the grade in terms of verifiable standards and visible performance does not bring a man to real security; it brings only anxiety and competitiveness. We, Jews who have become Christians, have made this move precisely for this reason; we put our faith in the Messiah, the one to whom the Jews have been looking forward as the clue to their history.

' "But," the objection will be raised, "if you people are so keen on your Christ that you throw overboard all the distinctions, especially the moral distinctions that lead to human dignity and noble character, aren't you making your Christ a conspirator in a programme of degradaion? Christian principles and Christian freedom may be all right for the sophisticated, but these Gentiles aren't saints yet, and they need a taste of discipline before they can be trusted. We must lift them up to our level, not pull ourselves down to theirs." No; the old understanding of things had to go. And if I now start to rebuild it, that can only mean that I feel guilty about the fact that I took part in its destruction. And I don't feel guilty about this, and I shouldn't, because the law itself tells me that it is not a sufficient guide and motivation. The law of Israel points away from itself to a time when people will live in terms of commitment not to a system but to a person. It points to a future. That future has now become present, and we are given the chance of either welcoming or discouraging, either accepting or rejecting, this new state of things. History has indeed made us what we are: but now we have the opportunity to make history ourselves, to take part in historical change. This is a whole new way of living, not just an exchange of one set of rules for another. In my journey to my present state, I had to let the law, our group tradition, do its worst with me, I had to be its implementor, its tool and its victim, without compromise. I tried to be really one hundred per cent an undeviating servant of the law and of my national tradition. And it killed me. It left me nothing which I could call "me"; it allowed power only to the destructive and negative drives in me; it turned these powers not only against my fellow-men but also against myself. But in dying by the law I found that I could still live even when the "I" that had been obeying the law had died. A new and real "I" came into being which could live in independence of that slavery to sectional tradition, an "I" which could be created new again for the God who is Lord of all men. I do not claim that this life is my own property to do what I choose with; I do not claim my activities to my own credit in a competitive scoreboard against other people. The dying which I have done is Christ's dying, his execution on a cross. And the life which I am living, a genuine physical life, is the life which he is able to live because he showed himself stronger than all the forces that destroy man and separate man from God and his neighbour. The whole history of the Son of God, his loving and his dying, have operated specifically for me. This is the one thing which I know absolutely about myself, that I am loved and do not have to produce a performance card to earn that love. This is all that really matters about me. The group tradition could not and cannot convince me of that: it can give me some security in terms of my success, if I manage to do better than other people, but it cannot give me the assurance that I am simply loved. I cannot go back on this conviction. If my place in God's favour comes because I deserve it through good performance, by getting a status of success or privilege over other people, then I am throwing Christ's gift back in his face; I say to him, "Jesus, your dying was a waste of time." '

I do not claim (this is John Davies speaking now, not Paul) that this paraphrase exhausts the meaning of these verses: the passage has some points of obscurity, and there can be differences of detail in interpretation. What we have here is not a doctrine but the clearest point in all his writing where Paul says 'This is me.' Nowhere is he more personal, nowhere is he more passionate. I would prefer to offer here an unbalanced interpretation which makes deep sense to me, rather than insert a whole series of academic pressure-relief valves labelled 'on the one hand' and 'on the other hand', which can never make deep sense to anyone.

'The Son of God who loved me and gave himself for me' is the strongest word of personal salvation. People who pride themselves on their concern for social and political issues often despise this emphasis; they call it pietism or individualism. But here is the root of political courage. Only a person who has been grasped by a gospel of his own deep valuedness will have the nerve really to confront the ideological idols which make people support inhuman policies. Evil policies do not appeal because of their theoretical consistency or their statistical verifiability; and those who seek justice need stronger motivations than theories and statistics in their struggle.

'The law' is a system which plays for safety. The appeal of 'the law' is essentially to that area of human nature that we know can be relied on – namely our unlovedness. Everyone can rely on the fact that everyone else has been inadequately loved and will behave accordingly. Partly to exploit this fact and partly to protect ourselves from its full effectiveness, we devise various systems of grouping by dissociation and of assessment of each other in terms of performance. All this is bound up with 'the law': it is a method of identifying ourselves in terms of those factors which stress our difference from other people, and which insist that we should characterize ourselves in dissociation from others.

Against all this, it is not enough for people to say, 'This is unjust' or to plan an adjustment of political and economic power. Nor is it enough for one group to say to another, 'Mend your ways.' What is needed is for someone – it could start with just one person – for someone to feel and to know, to sing and to shout and to mean, 'But by God I know that I *am* loved and that's what matters and everything else is a load of rubbish.' Paul knew that as an individual person his lovedness was not only the most important but also the most reliable thing about him, because the one who loved him had died rather than compromise it, and was alive to assert it. The love of Jesus is the most important political force in the world, not because it smoothes everything over and gets everyone together in a nice consensus, but because it releases a person to stop relying on his own unlovedness and on the unlovedness of others. The love of Jesus is permission to shout down the system; the love of Jesus makes you stand up to your visiting archbishop in the presence of the whole congregation and tell him that his behaviour is incompatible with the gospel.

For the gospel tells me that the most important thing about me is the love of God for me, and that my real status is not due to my ancestry or classification, my wealth or ability, my goodness or success, but to the justifying grace working out for me in the cross of Christ. And the gospel also states that this is the most important thing about my fellow-person, however different he may be from me in every other way. If I reject, as Peter did, another person's fellowship, if I allow the community of race to be more significant for me than the community of grace, I am abandoning all that Christ has given; I am abandoning my own central identity; I am abandoning Christ himself.

But the love of Jesus is not a soft option for the rabble-rouser. Certainly, Peter's behaviour was misleading and disgraceful; but it happened under an immediate pressure for compromise, and under-privileged people often understand and tolerate and forgive the clumsy, tactless privileged people who let them down from time to time. Peter is forgivable. The unforgivable would be a fake Paul. Christian commitment is not a matter of pillorying other people's compromises, of making mixed-up people squirm, of making bold confrontations, or of sounding off impressive personal testimonies about the love of Jesus. The love of Jesus is not just another formula. Either it really and deeply does motivate a person to see people in an entirely new way, and to act on this, or else it is the most dangerous deception of all. The man who claims to know that he is deeply loved must also be able to make the apparently opposite claim, that he has been crucified. The first claim, on its own, could be just euphoric froth; the other, on its own, could be a symptom of depression or paranoia. Paul makes both claims simultaneously; but he links both his crucifiedness and his lovedness to Christ.

In the next chapter, Paul goes into considerable detail about the meaning of Christ's crucifixion. But the first crucifixion which he mentions in his letter is his own. 'I have been crucified . . .' For Paul, the word 'crucifixion' would not be just a piece of conventional religious chatter. Paul was a Roman citizen. Indeed, some Christians think that he took his citizenship too much for granted, that he was insufficiently critical of the political and administrative establishment. However that may be, Paul was, above all, the preacher and theologian of the cross. And the cross, in his day, was not a gilded emblem standing between candles: it was the instrument of judicial execution, the weapon of counter-revolutionary violence, the symbol of imperialistic reprisal against a disenfranchised people's struggle for freedom. Paul not only has the nerve to proclaim a liberator who is identified by this badge of subversion: he first of all claims that he, Paul, Roman citizen, has himself been crucified, that he has experienced the punishment which was administered to convicted guerrillas. This is perhaps the most extraordinary of all the effects of his conversion. This is the measure of his liberation.

Further, Paul makes it clear that crucifixions did not end

with Christ; in a vital way they started with Christ, for Christ's disciples are crucified with Christ and after him. Christ's crucifixion, therefore, has not brought about our final liberation, nor has it abolished the power of the crucifiers. But Christ's crucifixion gives his disciples a model and a tool by which they can interpret their own crucifixions. His victory does not release us from our involvement with the evil in our own real world; but it gives us valid hope as we become involved and as we work out our own battles.

The conclusion of this argument is that the gospel of Jesus Christ is not only the gospel of man's liberation: it is the gospel of the liberation of God. God no longer has to look at man in terms of man's performance, measured against a set of rules. To look at man in that way is to look at him firstly in terms of his past, secondly in terms of his failure. Man is, at best, a high-jumper, the saddest of athletes because his last attempt is always a failure: the mind of the law gives credit to those who haven't done as badly as the rest. If we believe in a god like this, our religion will be an expression of our anxiety about our place in the status contest. And if our god is primarily valued because of his ordering of the affairs of the past, if he is seen primarily as the preserver of the inheritance of the past, our religion will be an expression of our own wish to lock people in definitions derived from the past, definitions of ancestry and definitions of moral standing. This is what a religion of law leads to. Anything which blurs the boundaries is dangerous. Forgiveness is as dangerous as the relaxing of racial barriers, for exactly the same reason. All this attitude imprisons God. He is allowed to see only man's guilt, man's past, and man's origin. The gospel of Jesus Christ is a gospel of divine liberation, of the liberation of God himself. God is freed to look at a man in terms of what that man can become; he can see him freed from the definitions and adjectives by which man has been restricted. Those who worship the God who is Father of Jesus Christ are committed to seeing their fellow-man through God's liberated eyes.

Law or Faith 3:1–14

1 You fools! Paul makes a sudden switch of style and temperature. He is neither polite nor gentle. He addresses the Galatians as people who are victims of some force which has interfered with their thinking processes.

But even at this point, Paul is not trying to devalue his readers; he is not trying to batter them into agreement or repentance. Who is responsible for this change of attitude, he asks? Somebody must be responsible. The eyes of the Galatians must have been spellbound by a sorcerer. They are victims of a conspiracy of evil, which is spreading this infection in an envious response to the attractiveness of the true gospel. These eyes which have become fascinated by the sorcerer are also the eyes before which Jesus Christ crucified had been advertised. Paul had held up Christ as a placard before these people, and their gaze had been held by the placard. Now they have allowed their eyes to switch to the sorcerer, and they have yielded not only their eyes but their minds to him.

Paul sets a firm limit to his role as missionary. His task, which we observe him performing in *Galatians*, is to make sure that people can see the truth and its implications. The missionary does not force people's minds: his task is to enable his hearers to take responsibility for what they hear; he does not try to get them to hand over responsibility for their beliefs and their consciences. He does not, like the sorcerer, play tricks with people's eyes. He holds up the placard. His task is to ensure that if people accept Christ they accept Christ and not some caricature of him, and that if they reject Christ they reject Christ and not some caricature of him. This is the way in which Jesus himself used his communication media. He spoke in parables. But, for him, the parable was not a device for compelling people to accept his arguments; it was a method of making people take responsibility for what they heard. It was a characteristically liberating form of communication (see Matthew 13:9–17).

2–5 Paul now appeals to the sense of logic which his readers have betrayed. He asks them what it was that really made the difference when they first became convinced about Christ. Was it something which hit your ears and made a new kind of sense to you? Or was it your success in obeying another set of rules? Have you missed the point of all your experiences? Can you really believe that all the most wonderful events of your life have happened because you were doing the right things and making the right noises and pressing the right buttons?

The choice here is not between two religious doctrines, but between two attitudes to the whole life of man. On the one hand is the attitude that life is in principle a mechanism, a set of sequences, a system of commerce and balance, of cause and effect, of stimulus and response. On the other hand is the attitude that life is basically a gift, a surprise. In the first attitude, it does not matter enormously whether the currency is moral or political or racial or religious; the effect on the personality is much the same. The gospel of Jesus Christ firmly asserts the second attitude. Further, the gospel is not just a theory; it has a living story to tell, of how a man who understood life as gift suffered the worst that could be done by those who insisted on life as system, and of how that man beat even the mechanisms of death.

6 And so Paul is brought to the fascinating figure of Abraham. Here is the man of faith, the man who twice received his son as a gift. Abraham received Isaac as a surprise of grace, firstly in his birth in his parents' old age, secondly in his deliverance at the place of sacrifice (see Genesis 15:1–6; 22:1–19).

Paul quotes the statement in scripture that Abraham had faith in God, and that because of this faith he was reckoned as a righteous man. The distinctive feature of Abraham was this attitude of faith, not the record of his moral achievement. But this is not to say that an internal disposition of the mind is sufficient. If an attitude is *only* internal, it is not an attitude of faith. Faith is something acted. Paul's whole argument is based on the very specific historical action of Peter in not eating with his Gentile brothers. Fellowship is action. Peter is an example of non-faith, and this is to be perceived not because someone has got a super encephalograph that can measure the inner recesses of the soul in wavelengths, but because of an uneaten bit of bread and a cold chair.

But the action by which faith is seen is not the kind of action which can be fitted into a system of law. It cannot be made into a universal rule, applying to all citizens. Abraham prepared his son Isaac as a sacrificial offering, in very particular circumstances. This was a specific way of showing trust in God who had the whole situation in hand, not only the situation of Isaac's individual safety but the situation of the whole future of Israel as a community. Abraham is able, as it were, to say in this action, 'Isaac is not *my* treasure, *my* only son, *my* hope. Isaac is God's. He is in the care of one who is both behind me and ahead of me. I can still go out not knowing where I am going.' Here is Abraham as the man of faith in his old age. Faith is not something which he has: it is his willingness not to have (see Hebrews 11 : 8).

The story of Abraham is not a moral example, to stimulate people to the attitude of surrender so that they, like Abraham, may be friends of God; this again is to legislate Abraham. Abraham did not surrender to God because some preacher had told him that if he did so God would love him and give him peace of mind. Nor did he surrender because he felt frightened, ineffective and alone, or because he had an urge to self-destruction which he could legitimize by turning it on to his most precious possession. These are signs of the sick and depressed and lawbound soul; there is no trace of them in the original story of Abraham, and nowhere do the New Testament writers fall into the danger of offering him as a moral example. Abraham is not an example in that sense. He is a model, a specimen. In him, we see how a man can behave if he is simply sure.

7-9 Paul's argument shows that the urgent question was 'Who are Abraham's descendants?' There was, of course, a strong body of people who felt that the question was answered as soon as it was asked. Abraham's descendants are the racial or ethnic group called the Jews: if you can prove your place in that descent, you are in: if not, you are not. For Paul's Gentile readers, however, there would be nothing but despair in this answer. But they believe that they have found another answer which will let them in, namely the answer that the descendants of Abraham are those who fulfil the discipline of the law of Moses. Paul insists that this will not do either, not because they are incapable of keeping the law, but because keeping the law has got nothing to do with being a son of Abraham. The thing which was characteristic of Abraham, the thing which made Abraham Abraham, was faith. It is those who start out from this position of faith who are Abraham's sons.

Again, we have to stress that this 'faith' is not just another alternative to the other two answers, another externally verifiable qualification. Paul does not say 'faith in God' or 'faith in Jesus Christ'. Even these phrases would give the wrong impression; they would certainly be dangerous for us modern Christians, after all our centuries of creed-making and testing of men by formulae. Paul does not say 'those who *have* faith', those who have *got* something which other men haven't. He says, 'those out of faith' – those whose starting-point is faith, those whose direction is determined by faith, those for whom faith is their base. Faith is not something picked up on the way as an extra possession; it is the propellant which moves you out on to your course.

Paul is saying something like this: all over the world, irrespective of ancestry or of cultural and legal systems, you will find some people who are basically accepting life as a gift, who are prepared to risk, who are open to the future, who go out into situations content not to know everything in advance, who are prepared to live without visible guarantees. These people are the real children of Abraham; what is truest about them is what was truest about him. Because his attitude to life is found in them, God told Abraham that in him all groups of people would find their blessing. It is this kind of attitude in people which enables them to see the significance of the gospel of Jesus Christ. The hearing that is of faith hears the gospel of Jesus Christ and realizes that it makes sense, realizes that what had been a rather undefined attitude of freedom now has a vigorous set of personal symbols, a shape and thrust that can be put into words in terms of the activities, the dying and the victory of one man. The gospel of Jesus Christ speaks to this attitude of faith; it calls it up into effectiveness, not only in the rather privileged few who happen to be predisposed towards this kind of attitude already, but also in people for whom the whole idea of 'faith' has been very latent and dormant. Those who hear the gospel of Jesus Christ in faith are drawn into the number of the people of faith, the children of Abraham.

10–12 The negative implication of Paul's argument is that the opposite kind of people are under a curse. Again, Paul does not call them people who obey the law, the particular law of Moses: he calls them 'those out of works of law'. They are people whose starting-point is working according to system or rule, those for whom this is their identity and their direction of life. Obviously, Paul is primarily thinking of those who commit themselves to a rigorous obedience to the law of Moses; but there are many other forms of legalism to which Paul's observations would apply just as critically. At this point, the Gentile identity of many of his readers is important. A person who is born within a culture like Judaism may well keep the law happily and freely because it is part of his background and to some extent comes naturally; this was presumably the case of the Jewish Christians in Jerusalem. A person who comes to such a culture from another one, and starts to insist on keeping the whole law in all its detail as a conscious exercise, shows more clearly that he has found a system to surrender himself to; his motivations are seen to be basically directed towards the establishing of a slave state; for himself he will be unlikely to discover the joyful freedom which is possible for the man to whom the law is a natural way of living. For men of faith are indeed found living and working within conditions which look rigid and systematic. A man can live within a strict discipline of culture or occupation and yet be creative and unanxious. Protestants are sometimes surprised to find that monks and orthodox Jews can be truly relaxed and free people. Poets and students of the humanities may discover the same about engineers and lawyers. The real difference with which we are concerned here has little to do with culture or occupation. In fact, to grasp the difference at all we must beware of all stereotypes which limit our perceptions of people.

The curse is not a magic formula, or the retaliation of an angry god. The curse is identified by the way it operates as an obstruction to blessing and to the free movement of grace. The law is a curse in so far as it makes duty the primary motivation of life. It forces us to put our hopes into *trying*. But, in a very important sense, the gospel of Jesus Christ saves us from the demand of trying to be good. This is not because goodness is no longer good, but because the effort to be good is essentially self-regarding. The law is a curse because, although it is a good thing in itself, and offers a good ideal, it draws a person to evaluate himself in terms of his own performance. It connives with his instinct to be anxious about his place in the moral competition, his level on the status-ladder. And this in turn connives with his tendency to see himself in dissociation from other people, to see other people as threats to his own position, or to find encouragement only in other people's failures which relieve this threat. Law then becomes valued as a method of detecting other people's faults and as a means for making them feel guilty. Guilty people can be held, tricked and manipulated; this plays straight into the hands of those who wish to retain the controls and to keep other people servile.

Paul was a dangerous man because he was not guilty. His arm could not be twisted: he could not be manipulated by many of the usual human fears. He was no longer in bondage to his own need for approval. He no longer felt that he had to be good in order to retain God's love. He was no longer a slave to conscience. Christ was not a new resource for enabling a man to be better than he otherwise would be, or to be better than his moral competitors. Christ was the one who had put all this kind of question into the past. Paul knew that he was not guilty, not because he had never incurred guilt but because he was overwhelmingly conscious of having been declared not guilty by one who had the power to do so. He was convinced that he was not guilty, not because he had suppressed his feelings of guilt but because he had been released by an undeserved acquittal. He was free from the curse. A community of people in the world who were equally convinced of their acquittal would be the most subversive force yet seen. They would defy most of the usual human distinctions; their responses would be impossible to predict or to manipulate. And that is what the church is supposed to be. It is supposed to be 'normal' – normal with Christ's 'normality'.

13 Christ became cursed by the law to release us from the curse of the law. In his manner of death, he associated himself with the revolutionaries of his day; he became a political, social and religious reject. By insisting on the crucifixion, and not merely the death, of Jesus, his preachers kept Christ's cursedness as an essential and conspicuous part of their witness. Through the cross, Christ had associated himself with everyone whom the system of law condemns. The cross was not a glory or a heroism for the Jewish people, it was a form of hanging, and thus any crucified person incurred the curse of the law in Deuteronomy (Deuteronomy 21:23). In Judea, crucifixions were so common that they could happen three at a time. In his death Jesus was joining the millions who have left life under a curse. There is nothing superstitious or magical in saying that a person who is hanged is cursed; it is a simple statement of the obvious.

A vital part of the curse of crucifixions, in the eyes of Jews, was that the crucified criminal was stripped naked. He had 'nothing to bless himself with' – no covering, no disguise, no insignia. Clothing was a blessing, and a good person would have a 'clothing of good works'. Jesus of Nazareth might have been able to claim a private innocence, a character unstained by individual sin. But the first Christian preachers do not seem to have stressed this very much. They were much more concerned to claim that he had shared and carried the burden of the guilty. He had not made his private innocence a badge of moral success. Law makes goodness a commodity to acquire for oneself in the moral competition; it makes goodness divisive. But Christ incurred the curse of the law; he identified himself not in distinction from sinners but in solidarity with sinners. A private innocence cannot save the guilty: it can only increase their distance and aliena-tion. Indeed, private innocence can be secured for certain only by those who isolate themselves from their fellow-men. Jesus was involved with the real world, with its compromises and ambiguities. We believe that he was sinless, not because he passed all the tests that morality and law can devise but because he was not bent away from his commitment to the love of God and the kingdom of God. And that kind of sinlessness cannot be objectively demonstrated to satisfy an ethical consensus.

To be crucified means nothing less than to be cursed as a sinner. And we proclaim a crucified Christ. If we find this distasteful, it is probably because we have got too used to thinking of 'Christ' as just another word for the private individual figure of Jesus. But 'Christ' is not just a personal name. 'Christ' means a belief and a vision concerning the nature of hope and deliverance. The Jesus-type of Christ demonstrated that the real hope for man is not in moving away from evil, either by pretending it isn't there or by trying to establish a private innocence whereby the best performers in the morality competition may succeed in gaining high status. 'Christ', according to the Christian gospel, means a liberation from that whole way of looking at oneself and at other people.

Valid hope is a Christ who will subversively disappoint all which 'the law' holds valuable. Hope is a freedom to be cursed. When the obstruction of the law has been dynamited away, the spirit which has been promised can flow out, infecting people with the attitude of faith, catching up and fulfilling all the latent attitudes of faith throughout the nations, where people have been basically orientated towards a Christ for whom they have been unconsciously waiting.

Thus the innocence of Christ is not an unchanging attribute of status for him; it is not his through privilege of origin. His innocence is dynamically proved through his function as victor over the role of sinner and the character of sinfulness which he took on himself. And this is what he shares with his people. He has shown his competence in handling the curse of evil and death. He does not invite us to return with him into an original condition of innocence: he invites us to share in a mastery which he has discovered in our own world of cruelty and confusion. (The above three paragraphs owe a lot to Martin Luther. He has several pages of powerful and passionate argument on these themes, on page 268 onwards of his *Commentary on St Paul's Epistle to the Galatians*, James Clarke, London, 1953.)

14 Mission is a reciprocal process. The mission of the church in Paul's day moved from a Jewish base towards people in Gentile areas. But the response of those who were being evangelized was also bringing completely new gifts to those who were doing the evangelizing. Because the Gentiles are sharing in the blessing of Abraham, Paul says, *we* (i.e. Paul himself and all other Christians, Jews and Gentiles) are receiving the promise of the spirit. For the first time they are living in terms of promise and gift rather than in terms of bargains and agreements. Involvement with Gentiles is, in a word, enabling Paul to live by grace. The flow of blessing is essentially two-way, not because the Gentiles are specially good but because this is the nature of the forces released by the event of the gospel.

The Law and the Promise 3:15-20

15-18 Perhaps it is this last reflection which restores the apostle to a good temper. He has called his readers fools: now, with emphasis, he calls them brothers, brothers through what Christ has done to both them and him.

The law, Paul states, has at best a secondary, temporary and intermediate character. Man does not start in law and then graduate to promise. Promise comes first; promise is the very nature of humanness; promise is the beginning and the end of existence. Promise is both caterpillar and butterfly, and law is merely the chrysalis. Law is adolescence, a temporary phase. When we take law as the permanent basis of life, we find that we reckon people's worth in terms of their comparative deserving. The valuable people are those who best fit our standards and get through all the various filters by which our culture selects people for privilege. So we become better at making comparisons than at receiving gifts, and religion becomes a means of sanctifying our competitiveness.

In his dealings with Abraham, God had established his character as promise-giver. Blessedness comes as a gift, an overflowing of generosity, and this is the unchanging character of God, which no amount of subsequent law-giving can alter. So, however hard we search for an acceptable method of identifying Abraham's descendants, we shall never succeed in finding the promised blessedness; for that comes only as a gift, not by any process which can be tied down. Any scheme of things which tries to tell us that the most important fact about us is that we are someone's descendants is ultimately part of the conspiracy against Christ. If I believe that I am what I am because of something which I automatically inherit from my forebears – be it wealth, culture, or race – I am refusing to be a child of promise. I am insisting on depreciating my own humanity.

19–20 Paul asks, 'Why law?' And he answers that law exists because of evil. It is an addition to the original design, and is intended to expose or control or counteract evil activity. It is valuable, therefore, as a device or tool or mechanism. But those who take law as their fundamental way of life or basic identity are condemning themselves to a bondage of gloom, because they are basing their security on the persistence of evil. In Christ evil has met its master, and law has only a limited usefulness. A life based on law appears superficially to be realistic; in fact, it is the way of despair.

Next, Paul recalls the story of how the law of Moses originated, how it was given by means of angelic agents and an intermediary or go-between. The presence of the angels emphasizes the distance between the giver and the receiver of the law. They emphasize the hierarchical system which at this point separates God from man and which therefore separates me from my origin, destiny and security. Then Paul introduces the figure of the mediator, Moses, who is so different in character and function from Abraham. Whereas Abraham is one of us, the first of the family to whom the promises were given, Moses functions as one who is distinct from us. The law requires that someone function as its mediator or agent. The promulgation of law always involves at least potential hostility: it asserts that there are two parties, and therefore there is a need for a go-between or reconciler. No such functionary is required in the case of a promise. To live in terms of law and to live in terms of promise are not just two different structures: they involve quite different ways of looking at other people. When a marriage is existing in terms of law, the husband is not living in terms of his identity and oneness with his wife: he is thinking, 'How would I make my claim against her in order to convince a judge?' He conducts an internal argument in himself which assumes at least two other personages over against himself, namely his wife and the imaginary judge. When the marriage is living in terms of promise, the husband identifies himself with his wife, and assumes their oneness; no one else's opinion is necessary; there is no place for a mediator. Paul is saying that where there is a mediator there can be no oneness. A mediator cannot be alone. If he is present, he makes God not absolutely one, but merely one of several parties. But God is by nature absolutely one. There is in God, in his role as promise-giver, an infectious oneness, just as there is in the promise-giving spouse. With God as promise-giver, there is no contract or bargaining, no need for an assessor or a judge, no appeal to an onlooker or interpreter. To move away from the area of promise into the area of law is to bring all those other agents in, and to crowd one's imagination with a mob of inspectors and zombies.

Christ is called our mediator. But this is not because he comes between God and man; rather he is himself both God and man, and the 'and' that loves God and man into one. Christ is himself an infectious oneness. In the Christian gospel, God does not *need* a mediator, and he does not even *provide* a mediator. The Christian gospel states that God is his own mediator. This is a more specific way of saying 'God is love.'

The Purpose of the Law 3:21–4:7

21–22 Can the law, which has come on the scene much later than the promise, contradict or overthrow or replace the promise as the sign of the permanent nature of man?

If the law contradicts the promise, then it is an unmitigated enemy; it must be destroyed. But this is too easy. The difficulty is that the relationship between law and promise can so easily be misunderstood. We can easily fall for the delusion that obedience to the law is a device for persuading God to fulfil his promises. But this is entirely the wrong way round. A much more valid sequence is when a person goes through a law-based phase of life and then starts to yearn for the romance of living according to a quite different sort of orientation. The law may be able to stimulate hope, but in itself it cannot bring life. That which brings life is gospel.

23 Law owes its origin to evil, and gives us a distorted view of evil. Law operates as a gaoler, by limiting the range of our vision. It encourages us to suppose that evil is the sum total of a lot of individual people's infringements of an endless series of regulations, and that it can be overcome by getting all these individuals to make greater and greater efforts to be good. The liberated person can see that evil is more like a massive conspiracy, and that it can be overcome by the infection of a whole new way of looking at things – for which the fundamental Christian symbol is death and resurrection.

Our imprisonment by law makes us unable simply to be good. If we do not have a really valid tool which can enable us to encounter evil and dig out a deep interpretation of it, the best that we can do is to clean ourselves up and make ourselves acceptable, by trying to be 'good'. But this is as frustrating as battering against the prison door. We require ourselves not merely to be good, but to be good enough today to compensate for yesterday's badness. So we settle for a standard of goodness which is lower than the standard that we know that we can attain, in order that we may have this surplus goodness. Our goodness is not done for the sake of goodness, but to enable us to balance our virtue-account. Each good action is then an awkward reminder that we have accepted an inferior standard. To compensate for this inferiority, we have to pay higher and higher prices, and make greater and greater sacrifices. In the first instance, we may pay for the sacrifice ourselves; but as the system takes hold, we shall be more and more organizing other people's sacrifices. We shall involve more and more people in our frustration. The deep agony is that we know that we *must* do what we know we *can't* do. We persuade ourselves that we are succeeding, by trapping more and more people in systems of benevolent cruelty; their suffering and their insecurity will show that we have been trying very hard. More and more people become used as the raw material out of which we try to manufacture our own security. This is not merely an individual pattern; it also causes widespread political and social cruelty, where vulnerable minorities or depressed majorities are imprisoned in restrictive systems, while the powerful swap their anxieties with each other about the latest form of the crisis.

When we live by faith, we can give up this urgent interest in being good; our security no longer depends on this kind of success. Not only does this make a vast difference to our own spirituality: it also frees us from the demand to implicate other people in the spiritual economics of our search for acceptability. And the political effects of this kind of change can be immense.

24 Paul describes the law as a temporary supervisor, set over us until the arrival of Christ. This supervisor or 'instructor' (the TEV's word) was a quite specific functionary in Paul's culture, a functionary who can be found in any society where there is a great gap in privilege between one section and another. He was a trusted slave to whom privileged parents would hand over most of the responsibility for the upbringing of their sons. His task was to prepare the boys for a life of freedom and privilege which he did not share. His duty was to be both severe and servile. He was both the tool and the operator of an educational system by which society reproduced itself.

Paul has just previously been speaking of the law as a gaoler. Now he speaks of it as educational supervisor. The kind of education represented by the servile supervisor is not a liberation but another aspect of our imprisonment. From both, Christ comes as liberator.

Christ does not discredit education; but he does shift the emphasis, so that the 'supervisor' element – the enslaving, servile style of education which emphasizes social distance and social classification – is made obsolete. This is part of what 'faith' is about, in Paul's terms; and it suggests a whole range of questions by which an educational system can be evaluated.

There are societies in which the educational system is rigidly designed to reproduce the imbalances within those societies: there, the servants of the gospel may discover methods of education for liberation, which will quickly attract the hostility of the powerful. There are other societies, like the British, where the immense variety of educational structure gives an impression of freedom and flexibility: but a structure which the powerful feel to be free and flexible may be experienced by the less privileged as merely a more flexible form of tyranny, a system against which you can never win: and your sense of frustration is worse than ever. Against all educational structures, even the most radical, we need to bear in mind the significance of the close association which Paul makes between law as educator and law as gaoler.

25 When the time of faith comes, the role of the supervisor falls away. Faith is maturity. The mature man is not merely prudent, well informed, experienced, and able to weigh up pros and cons. He is a man who can be surprised; he is a man who can receive gifts. God is the one who gives more than necessary: his land flows with honey as well as milk. His son gives himself in wine as well as in bread. Faith is being surprised by what God is and what he gives. This is the kind of faith which takes over where the law stops. This is the kind of faith which is mature, and to our upside-down kind of minds it can easily look like an absurd sort of youthfulness in old age.

26 In this faith, we move from being servants to being sons. The status of servants is limited: it is only because there are boundaries and contracts that the status of servant is tolerable and possibly productive. The status of son is unlimited: there are no contracts or boundaries, because there is no question of productivity. There is no real *purpose* in being a son or having a son. Faith, therefore, is something which operates to remove purposes and calculations; it enables a person to stand where he is without needing to and without being obliged to. And the curious condition of human nature, according to the realism of Christian belief, is that this precious unnecessariness is such a difficult thing for us to grasp that the whole mechanism of Good Friday and Easter was required to bring it within range. Thus, there may be a thorough misrepresentation of the gospel when earnest preachers and radical prophets batter us into servanthood by insisting on 'what the church should be doing'. There is certainly an urgent mandate that we seek the kingdom of God and his justice; at the same time, we have to watch out that we do not try to justify ourselves by our usefulness – to God or anyone else. The church celebrates its unnecessariness in the style of its worship and its meetings; and sometimes it ought to give a lower priority to its urgent concern about rationality and relevance, and be content to be an outpost of purposeless being-for-its-own-sake.

27–29 This leads us to a statement which is one of the high points of New Testament proclamation. The issue of 'Jew or Greek?' matters no longer, nor does the issue of 'slave or free?' Nor does the issue of 'male and female'. There is only one Christ, who is put on like a garment. In him, inside him, dressed in him, there can be only one person. The differences between human beings are no longer more significant than our common humanity; they no longer can claim the right to insist on their power to present a problem of 'Do I belong or don't I?' The differences have lost their power to exclude.

We need to realize that the fault is not in the difference but in the use which we make of the difference. People exist in a wide variety of forms. One could make, as it were, a long row of different people standing alongside each other, and never come to an end of the possibilities of variation. This is not a defect: it is part of the glory of humanity. The trouble comes when we convert this 'horizontal' spectrum of human difference into a vertical ladder of status. Then we are no longer asking the simple question, 'What sort of person is that?' but the anxious insecure question, 'Is that person above or below me in the system?' Immediately, the other person ceases to be important to me in his own right, and becomes important because of what his status tells me about my status. I need to have utmost clarity about this, and I will therefore seek to fix his identity and classification as rigidly as possible. I will see him in terms of those features in which he differs from me; and I will limit my own identity to those features which make me distinguishable from people from whom I want to be distinguishable. Mankind has endless skill in devising new distinctions. Radicals and conservatives alike delight in being able to claim a new discovery, a fresh tool of language or perception which can make other discriminatory tools look a little old-fashioned. But Christ confronts us with the distinction to end all distinctions – the distinction between those who are concerned about distinctions and those for whom this great anxiety is abolished.

The features which matter most in establishing distinctions are based in the past. A racialist society, for instance, idolizes the past and is frightened by the threat of change. The past has decided a person's classification; it has decided his place in society, and has given him his appropriate value. His parentage has decided how acceptable his language or accent will be, and the fellow-humans to whom he will be a threat. The determinisms of the past are far more decisive than any possibilities for change in the future. It is no accident that a racialist society is likely also to be a very unforgiving society. Those who are afraid of change attach great importance to sin. If a person has offended, this fact becomes eternally and ineradicably significant about him. His past offence determines his present character. Forgiveness would confuse this identity and is not to be encouraged.

Paul identifies three kinds of difference. The difference between Jew and Greek is ethnic and cultural, that between slave and freeman is political, that between male and female is sexual. But these three pairs of differences all serve the same purpose: they have the effect of ministering to a need to make vertical distinctions of status. The ethnic and cultural distinction between Jew and Greek would be valued as a difference of status, just as the political distinction between slave and freeman would be valued as a difference of status. And, in the same way, the difference between the sexes can be valued primarily because it is another method of deciding who is to have power and who is not. In such a case, a person may need a kind of major conversion in order to value sex erotically.

The attack on racialism is an ideological camouflage unless it attacks the political assumptions about power which enable racialism to thrive. The oppression of the blacks is not caused by racial consciousness but by a power structure in which racial difference can be used to explain and justify the distinctions of status. The abolition of racial consciousness, on its own, would merely have the effect of absorbing a few privileged members of the oppressed group into a status-system devised for the benefit of the oppressors. (From the South African situation, there is an excellent exploration of this problem in Mokgethi Motlhabi's essay 'Black Theology and Authority', in *Black Theology*, edited by Basil Moore and published by C. Hurst, London, 1973.)

Paul is saying that this whole way of seeing oneself and other people is done away in Christ. In so doing, he is not merely commending a general truth; he is actively renouncing his own upbringing and conditioning. He rejects his own place on the status-ladder, and the mechanisms which have given him this place. For, in his cultural tradition, he would have been encouraged from earliest years to give thanks that he was not a Gentile or a slave or a woman. He is able to make this universal proclamation about the unity of humanity in Christ, not because of his superior powers in reasoning, speculation or metaphysics, but because he had learned something new and revolutionary about his own identity.

There is a further detail in Paul's language here. He says, 'There is no such thing as Jew *or* Greek, there is no such thing as slave *or* free.' Paul's third pair of distinctions is different. He says, 'There is no such thing as male *and* female.' The man/woman issue goes far deeper than the other two. It is not fundamentally a problem of classification at all. The man/woman issue is not only a 'man-or-woman?' kind of question: it is the dilemma of two beings who are designed to be a unity, but who in their very co-existence represent the most primal kinds of hostility. The 'and' represents a division which is all the more painful because it can also represent a unity. The work of Christ is something far greater than patching up the angers and stupidities of the Galatian church: Christ is overcoming the basic hostility at the heart of mankind. To express the matter in this way is not mere mythology. Nothing is a more efficient conveyor of the infection of evil from generation to generation than the hostilities between parents. It is from our experiences with them that very many of our motivations are built into our personalities, such as the motivations which make us so concerned about our place and our status that we feel under compulsion to insist on the 'Jew-or-Greek?' and 'slave-or-free?' kind of questions.

We have used our gift of sexual identity as a means to restrict our gift of power. Power, the mandate to be responsible for the rest of creation, is a gift to the whole of humanity and if we restrict it to a subsection of humanity we lose our hold on it. Our culture has tended to reserve overt power for males, and to divide humanity into people and females. 'He' can mean 'he-or-she', but 'she', in the norms of English language, can't mean 'she-or-he'. And we have sanctified this bias in our thinking by using heavily masculine imagery in our talk about God (although perhaps the old custom of calling God 'He' rather than 'he' shows that we realize the inadequacy of the straight pronoun). The healing of our disordered understanding of sexual identity is part of the salvation of the whole humanity, and it is not achieved yet. Paul himself was not outside the problem. He did not succeed in consistently applying the practical implementation of his deepest perceptions, when he came to give advice about the position of women in church or society, for instance. But it is easy to be consistent when your fundamental perceptions are conventional; Paul's perceptions at this point were as radical and unconventional as any in the history of thought or of politics and derive directly from his conviction of what Christ fundamentally means.

This ultimately goes back to the person of Jesus himself. In Jesus, people can and do find a model of humanity which bridges the divisions of sex and race and culture. In the gospel story his role and activities are defined not by his sex or culture-group, but by his freedom and passion for the truth about God and man. Gentiles, slaves and women have been able to feel that he is one of us. And when they do this, he nerves them to attack the disorder of a society which prefers the part to the whole. The gospel is that there is one Christ, one only for all people. He was a Jewish male. We hear of him largely through the writings of Jewish males: but they stress his capacity to defy this kind of categorization. They tell how in his lifetime he was more human than his culture would tolerate. And so non-Jews and non-males can find in him their model and their pattern.

We have just noted that the role and activities of Jesus were, according to the gospel, not primarily determined by his sex or culture-group. There is one obvious exception; Jesus was circumcised. This is important, because it is the point where it is made absolutely clear that, like each of us, Jesus was a child of a particular community. If this were not so, he would be more alien, not less alien, to the rest of us. But it is precisely at this point that, according to Paul, our following of Jesus depends on our not imitating him. Only half the human race, at most, can be circumcised in the way that Jesus was circumcised. If discipleship involves circumcision, the whole programme of rebuilding humanity collapses. As we see in *Galatians*, the argument about circumcision takes us into the most subtle aspects of human identification. But this should not blind us to the very simple, basic proposition which cannot be philosophized away, that no special privilege attaches to the physical accident that one has been born with a foreskin.

Paul has stated in the previous verse that we participate in this character of Christ through baptism. It may seem inconsistent for Paul to speak of the abolition of barriers and classifications and then to say that we associate with this achievement by undergoing a very special kind of ritual. Is not baptism a new kind of insignia, a badge of membership of an identifiable in-group? Does not this create an 'in-or-out?' situation as specific as the 'Jew-or-Greek?' situation?

But baptism has to be seen as the servant of the work of Christ, a method of applying the principle established in Paul's statement that in Christ the distinctions are done away. Baptism, if it is insignia at all, is the insignia of those who renounce insignia. As with Christianity itself, the importance of baptism is its unimportance. It is a strange, double-edged tool, which cuts those who try to use it to cut others. A person who is baptized is baptized into an in-group which is committed to the de-throning of all the idols which cause in-groups to form. It is surely no accident that, compared to religious and cultural initiation ceremonies old and new, baptism is in principle the most absurdly simple event. Of secret formulae, arcane passwords, complicated rituals and elaborate paraphernalia there is no end. Christ's simple secret is that you join God by getting wet.

4:1–2 Paul catches up again the theme of the temporary character of law. Until an heir comes of age he has only the status of a slave. The heir's coming-of-age is part of the father's programme of promise. The operation of this inheritance does not depend on the death of the testator but on the maturing of the heir. In our present culture an inheritance is something which an individual gets when a previous owner dies: this is bound up with our individualist understanding of property and land-tenure. In the Old Testament, Paul's background, the inheritance characteristically means the corporate possession of the group: the individual gets his share of it not in virtue of his father's death but in virtue of his entry into membership of the community (see Numbers 33: 54, etc.). The minor is like a slave; he is not in the adult com-munity; he has no real identity of his own, no power to perform responsible acts. He can act only through people who supervise and control his person and property; it will be their names rather than his which appear in the place appointed for his signature.

Slavery is a system in which a person has no value except as a functionary, in terms of his productivity; it is a system in which one group of people has the power to decide the value to be placed on other people. Redemption is what happens when a person is removed from this market and from this method of valuation; redemption abolishes the absolute right of the rich and powerful to decide a person's value in this way. The boundary between slave and non-slave is abolished; the slave ceases to be a slave, and in due course slavery itself ceases to be. Christian faith began to achieve this in a cultural setting where the best philosophers, politicians and lawyers defended slavery as a valuable institution. The battle is far from being finished, even in our so-called Christian cultures. There is little point in devising liturgies which give thanks that we are delivered from the slavery of sin, unless we are committed to seeking, for all people, deliverance from the sin of slavery. (For examples of how those whom we call the wisest and best from Greek culture were unable to see anything wrong with slavery, see J. B. Lightfoot's *St Paul's Epistles to the Colossians and Philemon*, Macmillan, London, 1890, p. 309.)

Paul's imagery of guardians and trustees does suggest that the testator has actually died, or at the very least that he is significantly absent. Certain debates a few years ago made the phrase 'Death of God' familiar. But these obituary-writers got their timing mixed up and missed some of the real subtleties of the human experience that Paul hints at here. For Paul, God's death took place not with the arrival of scientific technology, nor even in the crucifixion of Jesus. The death (or at least the removal) of God took place at the time when man came under the domination of guardians and trustees, when man came 'under law'. 'Law' talks a lot about God: it quotes God as the validator of its constitutions, the guarantor of its threats and the executioner of its condemnations. But this is God in his deadness, in his absence. The period of the death of God is the phase between the moment when the heir comes under law and the moment when he becomes a son. The death of God, therefore, is the time not of man's maturity but of man's adolescence. During that period, the chances are that there will be a lot of talk about God and a lot of anxiety about authority, expressed in either compulsive obedience or compulsive revolt. When we shout at God we inevitably demonstrate our sense of his distance from us. When God is closer, there may be less to say about him, and our voice can be quieter; man will have 'come of age'.

3–5 There has been much argument about what Paul means by the term 'ruling spirits' (*stoicheia*). Basically, the word means the letters of the alphabet, arranged systematically like 'ABC'. Paul claims that in our minority we were enslaved to the *stoicheia* of the universe (or of the world). It seems that he is using this term to suggest the elemental pressures and anxieties which make people attach great importance to fulfilling the systematic details of rules and regulations; and perhaps he also means the kind of pressure which makes people enthusiastic for systems of control and classification which impose a rigid order of precedence according to the determinisms of 'fate' or culture or religion or ancestry. 'ABC' is an excellent device for getting letters individually visible, precisely because the letters are arranged in the alphabet in such a way as to avoid any hint of their use in words. Indeed, according to James Thurber, the English dictionary can offer only one specimen of the letter-sequence '. . . abc . . .', namely the word 'dabchick' (see his *Alarms and Diversions*, Penguin, Harmondsworth, 1962, p. 349).

One aspect of the *stoicheia*, which Paul picks up a few verses later, is that the law has become a form of bondage to a calendar, a dependence on the movements of stars and planets. History very easily comes to be seen as the operation of a mindless destiny, or the repeating of an endless cycle of anniversaries and commemorations. These are valued because they reinforce what we already know and affirm the meaning of the past. A commemoration is a duty rather than a surprise. Paul has several times noted the temporariness of the era of the law; it operated *until* a new state of affairs broke in. Christ has not merely brought in a new series of events to replace the old: he has delivered us from the weariness and dutifulness associated with the idea of history which is shaped primarily by the cyclical pattern of commemorations. He has given a meaning to history by coming in at its mid-point. If Christians engage in commemorations, the purpose should be to enable us to identify more clearly the Christ who is born *today* and who is risen *today* – the new Christ who is gift and surprise.

The time came when the old system of law had to give way before the implementation of the promise, which had been the guarantee of man's true destiny from the beginning. When the fullness of time had come, Paul says, God sent forth his son. The term of man's adolescence had been completed. The period of adolescent attitudes had run long enough for it to be recognized as such, long enough for us to be able to identify the hopes which he comes to fulfil and the disorders which he comes to attack. He comes not when the world has become good enough to deserve his presence as a reward, but when conditions had developed in which his coming would precipitate the sharpest crisis.

This understanding of 'the right time' accords with Paul's imagery of the maturing of the individual person. For most of us, the 'coming of age' is not an entirely pleasant and successful process. It is the shift from being an overgrown child to being a baby person. It is a new birth into a whole array of new relationships, into a situation where we are not cushioned from the effects of our mistakes, and into a range of responsibilities, pains and ecstasies compared to which adolescence is a very dull game. We look back nostalgically to adolescence as a time when some kinds of success came much more easily than in our maturer years. We can see that the cultural developments which have taken place in the context of Christianity have brought crises and dangers to the world which it never knew before: and the same is likely to be true of the individual.

God is one who sends. He has sent his son into the world; he sends the spirit of his son into our hearts.

Without apology or hesitation, Paul uses language which asserts that God is not where we are, that he is distant and other. The idea of a remote God has come in for serious criticism in the last few years, and rightly so. But we cannot chop out from the scripture the great themes and images of a God who sends. The apostolic God works all through the Bible, bringing always a new critique, an invasion from outside the normal routine of things. It is unrealistic to try to get rid of the imagery of God's movement towards us and of our dependence on what comes from outside. Our tendency to do this is often linked to a feeling that we must think according to the norms of a scientific world-view. This notion of the earth's internal self-sufficiency and independence has so rooted itself in our consciousness that it comes as a real jolt to realize that this earth is not, in fact, self-sufficient, that all energy is derived from a structure which is remote and separate from it, namely the sun. The clearing-away of non-valid forms of dependence now makes clearer than ever the significance of our real dependence. If we seek to remove this imagery of dependence from our consciousness and from our theology, we shall simply starve ourselves of our natural source of energy, of renewal and of power for change. It is no accident that the period when theology was becoming most embarrassed about a transcendent, distant God has also been the time of unprecedentedly rapacious use of the earth's natural resources. When the church fails to proclaim this alien God of righteousness who stands over against the world as critic and deliverer, it is in effect supporting the systems of exploitation and oppression.

The Son of God was sent, and born of a woman. Whatever the reasons for the details of the story of the birth of Jesus, one of the most important effects of the story is that Jesus is known as the son of his mother. I, and millions like me, owe our surnames to the assumption that male ancestry is supremely important. The title 'Son of Mary' is practically unique: it recognizes the relationship in which human structuring actually takes place, an area which contemporary male-dominated politics, economics and even educational design, almost entirely ignore.

The son is sent to a specific place. If God is to be real, he has to be local, even if this presents problems to the bureaucratic mind which prefers to see things globally. It is not enough to say that Jesus is the first 'world citizen'. Before he can have that kind of status, he has to be a child of a particular mother, product of a particular culture. Paul does not state that the Son of God was born under *the* law, he says that he was born under law.. He was born into an authority-system and culture-pattern. To be born 'under law' is the universal human spiritual condition; it is the counterpart of being born 'of a woman', which is the universal human physical condition. Just as Jesus could not be born except of a specific woman, so he could not be born except under a specific law.

By being born of *a* woman, born under *a* law, the Son of God shared the condition of all who are born of all women, and all who are born under all law. This identity now takes precedence over the specific relationships under which he was born. This enables God to identify people of other human and cultural families as his sons. It dethrones tribal and cultural identities from having determinative power in human communities. We, Jews and Gentiles, are sons together. Previously, 'our' identity was shaped by the contrast between those who were children of Israel and those who were not children of Israel: now it is shaped by our common status as children of God himself, who is creator and critic of Jew and Gentile alike. Previously our identity was shaped by a biological and cultural inheritance which belonged to us by accidents of parenthood and upbringing: now it is shaped by a specific deliberate policy of God who has chosen us as his children, by the process called adoption, a process which unites people of different origins into one family.

6–7 A son's coming-of-age does not depend on his own moral or technological competence. The sign that man has really come of age is that something has happened to the image of father. A man comes of age when father is wholly father, with no admixture of tyrant or owner, when father's image is freed from its threats, hostilities and jealousies. Many of us never quite 'grow up', in this sense: we remain adolescent and irresponsible, allowing father to act as censor to our consciousness.

Man can be said to have come of age when his image of God is united to a valid image of father, an image which is liberating and whole. Maturity in this sense cannot be organized or bargained for; it cannot be part of the system of law; it cannot be purchased in the market-place or earned in the commerce of slavery. It somehow has to just happen; but it does not happen spontaneously. The Christian gospel states that it has happened, through the specific policy of God in sending his son into the world. The son was sent to discover and to realize what genuine sonship is like, and thereby to demonstrate the character of God as the 'normal' father. Jesus makes it possible to believe in 'whole' fatherhood. The first Christians found themselves believing in this kind of father, and celebrated their belief by describing Jesus as 'Son of God'. When we are in the same room with someone who is conducting a telephone conversation, we can observe the attitudes and words of that person; and from him we can get some idea of the character of the unseen person at the other end of the line. In the same way, we have evidence of the character of Jesus, and from his behaviour we can get some idea of what the Father is like.

What is more, the friends of Jesus found that they were being infected with his kind of attitude towards the Father. Because of this, they became passionately concerned about the fellowship, and unconventionally casual about human categorizations. And again, the most adequate language to describe this liberation was to say that God had sent the spirit of his son into their hearts.

The spirit enables the Christians to use Jesus' unique form of addressing the Father, 'Abba'. The first Christian communities found that they had the same sort of access to the Father that Jesus had claimed. They had absorbed his attitudes and used his language.

But there is an important difference of connotation between 'Abba' and 'Father'. There is nothing quite corresponding in Greek to 'Abba'. 'Abba' is, in Hebrew, the first meaningful sound that a baby makes. It is not the ordinary word for 'father' in general use. It is a peculiarly intimate term, and if there is a sound in English which approaches its significance it would be 'Dad' rather than 'father'. But the whole point of such a word of affection and intimacy is that it is destroyed if you try to legislate it. You can't make a liturgy out of 'Dad'. You can't ask or require people to use it. It cannot be a new rule to replace the old one. It is not a human enterprise or organization that produces this language: it is the spirit of the son which speaks like this, the spirit which God has sent into our hearts. To call on God as 'Dad' is something which happens to us, not something which we contrive or practise. Genuine communication always owes a great deal to the person to whom it is addressed; he enables the communication to take place. Prayer is a matter of God's initiative, not of our organizing. And when such prayer happens, it is a sign that we are sons. We have become involved in the adult experience of communication. We have grown up. We have passed through the crises of adolescence into maturity, and this is signified by the fact that we use a form of address to Father which looks almost infantile. The sophisticated claim 'God is dead' is really less adult than the childish claim 'God is dad.'

The knowledge that God is Son as well as Father makes a deep difference to the way that the whole image of God registers with us. Disorders in our understandings of God often derive from our disordered relationships with our fathers. God shows himself as a source of healing at this point, not by facing us with new demands or behaviour-patterns but by disclosing that he is more than father. He is not limited to the character of father, even of father as maturely understood in the perceptions of Jesus. God discloses that he is himself at the other side of the father/child tension; he is identified as child as well as father. We, therefore, may quite realistically expect to find as much insight into the nature of God from our relationships with our children as we discover from our relationships with our fathers. God is knowable at both sides of the conflict, and in himself overcomes this conflict. Our address to God as Father can be mature and whole and valid, because we are addressing one who is also child.

This whole shake-up of our understanding of God is highly germane to Paul's general purpose in *Galatians*. Beyond all the other categorizations, discriminations, resentments and conflicts, the basic one which gives power to the others is the parent/child tension. The Christian gospel attacks this basic disorder at its root, and offers power and clues for its cure. In western culture, this disorder is on such a large scale that it is scarcely visible; it is enabled and stimulated by most elements in our economic and social system, and therefore we may find peculiar difficulty in perceiving the implications of the gospel at this point. But if this fundamental relational disorder can be tackled, other ones, such as the hostilities between cultures and races, should be comparatively easy to cope with.

The minor son resembles a slave, but only temporarily. He can look forward to growing out of his adolescence; but the slave himself can become a son only by a very basic change in his status, in the extremely unlikely event that he will be adopted into the family. The slave earns his place in the household by fulfilling certain functions. The son owes his place to the simple fact that he is son. He is accepted in the household not because of his activities, his diligence or faithfulness, but simply because he is. Modern emancipatory society has claimed that a person's status ought not to depend automatically on his parentage; we now identify ourselves by the function which we contribute to our fellow-men, rather than by our ancestry. To be a fitter or a nurse is more important than to be a black man or a gentleman. Good. But a person is most able to exercise his function within society in a liberated and responsible way only when his basic identity is secured in a status which does not depend on his performance. He is merely contributing more to the world's disorder if he uses his functional capacity as a means for securing a status in competition with other status-seekers. Just to shift from a class-based society to an achievement-based society may do more harm than good. The meritocracy believes that a person's value is determined by what he is able to produce; and this in turn is demonstrated by what he possesses and by how much he is able to consume. This is a shift from one slavery to another; it is a form of justification by works.

The slave cannot allow himself to fail, because failure in role or function incurs loss of status. Our modern achievement-centred society makes freedom possible for the healthy, the competent, the successful; it vigorously segregates the unsuccessful, the incompetent, and the misfit, and allows them far less place than they get in society in less success-ful cultures. It makes us terrified of failure. In order that success may carry some sense of privilege, our society has to ensure that a distinct minority will be failures. In some areas (at present this seems to be most conspicuous in areas with a significant proportion of black people) it can be predicted that many children will be on the educational scrap-heap even before they start going to school. These people are condemned to one kind of enslavement. But those who are in bondage to a success-image are also enslaved. The slave – and the slave-church – will seek to avoid the situations of real demand, where failure is almost certain. If a thing is worth doing, it's worth doing badly; but the slave won't see this. The son can risk failure and can risk death, because he owes his status to something that is not his to manipulate or organize. The slave-church will almost certainly get more impressive results by stressing the need for its members to improve their performance as servants of God. It will retain the members who are a credit to it, and filter off the misfits and the un-clever. It will concentrate on the activities at which it has proved its success; but by avoiding failure, it will fail to be the one thing that it is designed to be, a community of the sons of God.

Paul's Concern for the Galatians 4:8–20

8–11 Paul's readers have been redeemed. They have been taken out of the system of slavery, and they have come to know and to be known in a new way. But to live without insignia and classifications makes people feel exposed and deprived of landmarks. The Galatians' ambition to be circumcised is a reversion; it is a renunciation of freedom; it is a refusal of God's mandate to man to be an explorer, to take the opportunities to live within the widest boundaries.

Paul has reason to be deeply alarmed at this situation. It is not simply that his readers are disobeying him or departing from his teaching. The deeper problem is that his work has somehow produced not Christian commitment but frustration, weariness and depression. It is in these circumstances that people try to find a solace in a religion of scrupulosity and unproductive activity. In short, his readers are heading for a breakdown; their behaviour is not merely disappointing or disobedient: it is symptomatic of a serious inner disorder.

12–16 Because of what God has done in Christ, Paul is able once more to address these Galatians as 'brothers'. On the basis of their membership of the one family, Paul and his readers have become like each other. Paul asks them to act on the one fact that is true about both of them, that they are being brought into relationship with each other. 'I am becoming as you are,' he says; 'I beg you therefore to become as I am.' At present you are insisting on moving away from me, you are denying a relationship which is being made between us. I am being brought into an inclusive fellowship of faith and away from an exclusive, sectional system of classifications and regulations; as you move towards such a system you are moving away from me. I am coming to where you used to be, but you are moving to where I used to be. If this happens, we are no longer brethren.

In the past, he says, you did not treat me wrongly; you accepted me in spite of the fact that my physical condition must have been a temptation to you to ignore and spit at me. You received me as one sent from God; you received me as Christ Jesus. Paul has been sent into a strange area, and found brothers. Their reception of Paul as a sent person represented something of the manner in which Jesus Christ comes as a sent person.

Paul's mission was further validated by the fact that he was put into the power of these brothers as soon as he arrived. There was something about him which was naturally repulsive. While they were receptive to the true gospel they were receptive to him across this barrier of

physical unattractiveness. Part of Paul's character as a
sent person, in this instance, was that there was plenty of
opportunity for him to be rejected; he did not retain the
controls, and he became under obligation to them.

But now the Galatians have changed their commitment: they have identified Paul as their enemy. Paul
complains that he is puzzled by this, that he has lost his
way. It is absurd that people should be attracted by something that is so perverse. Reasoning and demonstration
are no sure remedy, for the disorder is itself anti-rational.
This is very close to the heart of the nature of evil; the
more it displays its destructiveness and illogicality, the
more attractive it is. Evil reverses this and makes maturity
infantile.

17–18 Paul's opponents are playing on the Galatians'
anxiety about their own identity. Evil searches around
for a soft spot of insecurity and drills away at it. 'They
want you,' Paul says, 'but not in the right way: they wish
to exclude you so that you may be more attracted to
them.' This is a very simple stratagem to employ against
any group of people who are sensitive to this kind of
anxiety. The sense of being excluded is a very painful
one and is calculated to make people servile. The victims
of this stratagem are made to feel inadequate and un-
qualified, and so they are stimulated to seek the qualifications possessed by those who are qualified. This puts
them under the domination and control of those who are
qualified and who decide what the qualifications are.
There is no sense of equalizing or of fellowship in this
process, but only a sense of continuing indebtedness and
inferiority. By such means, the disadvantaged are kept
in a position of disadvantage, and the distances are
maintained. Real genuine separation is far more healthy
than this tantalizing, conditional excludedness which
exaggerates the importance of detailed qualifications,
sets each man against his neighbour, and breeds lick-
spittles and informers.

19–20 Paul's policy has been to encourage Christian
groups to grow quickly into maturity by withdrawing his
presence from them. He has been anxious to avoid

over-dependence and has left them to find maturity in their own resources. Previously, he has been mother to them (incidentally, this imagery shows that he was able to see the male and female roles with some flexibility). They have grown from embryos into the formation of Christ, and he has brought them through the crises of birth and infancy. But then, his departure has weakened their security, and in their anxiety they have attempted to find a new kind of security, a security based not on the utterly undeserved acceptance by mother but on a system of earning and qualifications. This makes him feel that it would be a good thing if they were back in the womb again, so that the process of the formation of Christ in them could be done over again. He wishes that he could be present with them, and be a maternal figure of acceptance again.

The Example of Hagar and Sarah 4:21–31

21–23 In a situation of this kind, a person in Paul's position has to look around for approaches by which he can speak to the condition of his readers. Ordinary reasoning is not likely to be much use at such a time. Paul could probably have out-argued anyone in the district, but that would hardly help. If he succeeded in persuading his hearers, they would submit to his reasoning, acknowledging that he was the better reasoner; if he failed, they would be conscious of the fact that he had all the arguments on his side, but nevertheless they weren't going to be shaken. In either case, they would be left feeling stupid, and the gap between Paul and themselves would be wider. Paul knows that they cannot save themselves by being ritually or behaviourally 'right'; he also knows that he cannot save them by being intellectually 'right'. So he has to search around for a way of relating to their emotional life. He looks for a picture or model or story that will 'ring bells' with them.

The elaborate discussion of Abraham's wives and sons does not 'ring bells' with us and there is no use pretending that it does. It is a poor set of symbols for us, because it does not relate directly into our emotional life or our mythology. But evidently Paul thought that it would speak to his readers, captivated as they were by the Jewish religious tradition. From this tradition, Paul is able to derive three contrasts, between two types of motherhood, two types of relationship, and two types of city.

Hagar-style motherhood is the style which stresses the process that is according to the flesh. This does not mean just the sexual process: it means the whole process of observable, predictable development. The slave-state of Hagar's son is to be seen in the fact that he is *only* the child of his parents; he is *only* the product of the natural process; he is seen only as a predictable unit within a mechanistic system. This mother, Hagar, represents a motherhood of cause-and-effect; she is only what her origin allows her to be. She is a slave, and her slavery is communicated to her son.

The slave Hagar is treated as a thing. She is a prostitute; her body is used to satisfy a lust, not an erotic lust but a lust to secure an offspring. She is a tool by which Abraham tries to implement his thwarted ambitions; she is a cipher in a scheme of political manipulation, a component in a device of human engineering. Abraham himself tries the way of non-faith; he experiences the disappointment and despair which come to those who trust in mechanisms and who seek freedom in the future by practising slavery in the present. Where a woman is enslaved to produce a son, that son is likely to be a slave also. He will be seen as the product of a successful scheme; he will have to conform to the role for which he has been designed. Organization man will breed organization child.

The opposite to Hagar is the 'free woman'. Her son was born according to a promise. This does not mean that his birth bypassed the sexual process. It means that the birth of this son, Isaac, is seen as something more than a natural event. He is something more than the product of genetic mechanisms – or of political mechanisms. He is the product of no one's schemes and ambitions. He is not born 'by the will of the flesh'; he is born free. He is a gift, a surprise. He breaks the bounds of expectation, and is accepted as a wonder and a joy. This kind of mothering is free to allow the son to be free, to

be unpredictable, to be more than what his origin allows
him to be.

24–26 So there are these two types of relationship or
covenant. The Hagar-style covenant is that which is based
on the law of Sinai. The promises of this covenant are
conditional: '*If* you do this and that, *if* you keep the
rules, *if* you are good, God will keep his part of the
bargain, God will love you.' But we can never grow to
maturity if our acceptableness and membership are only
in proportion to our success in 'being good'. We cannot
be free if we are continually checking to see whether our
goodness is sufficient to gain the approval of a parent-
figure. Only the unconditional relationship of the free
mothering can nurture a responsible conscience.

And there are two types of city. Hagar/Sinai corres-
ponds to the contemporary Jerusalem; it is in the same
category. The bondage of Jerusalem, in Paul's day, was a
profound spiritual condition, as well as a notorious
political fact. Jerusalem was a community which could
have become the centre of the world's peace, it could have
been a focusing point for the development of a common
human culture. But Jerusalem – 'the contemporary
Jerusalem' – could not face the surprise of being more
than it knew itself to be: it missed its chance.

There is the other Jerusalem, the Jerusalem that is
above. The true city is an assembly of people of different
abilities and specialisms, who live by supplying each
other's needs. In this kind of community, distinctions
based on ancestry or inherited status obstruct co-operation: they are strictly uncivilized. The true city is free to
be mother of all her citizens, and enables them to grow
in freedom. Membership of the city, the polis, is a political experience, and the co-operation needed for the city
to be true to its nature is a political skill.

Paul is not talking about a distant, purely 'spiritual'
city, in some remote state beyond death. The first city
he mentions is certainly described as 'the now Jerusalem'
– the Jerusalem that is currently identified by that name.
The opposite of this, however, is not the 'then' Jerusalem
in the distant future, but the 'above' Jerusalem which is
of a higher character. This 'superior' Jerusalem has given

us birth as our mother, and therefore was in existence before us. It is not just an object of hope for a future life beyond death. The 'above' Jerusalem is a reality now. It is a present community which we can share and proclaim, a community which we can now experience and which has its own political bite; it is a community brought into being by the resurrection of Jesus.

27–31 Paul sees that the whole issue centres around the question of security. The Galatians feel that their condition is one of inadequate support and identity. You feel desolate and barren, Paul says; you seem to have no figure of support at your side and you seem to be much less productive (of good works, success, social credibility, etc.) than the communities which live in terms of classification. But God is the master of history, the reverser of roles, and the guarantor of his people's freedom. Ultimately, history is on your side, if God be God. Brothers, Paul says again, stressing the union in Christ between himself and his readers; you have been born, like Isaac, out of a situation of deadness and hopelessness. The only explanation for your existence is that a promise has been fulfilled in your birth. Your being is made possible by a power which far exceeds the routines of the natural process or the powers which people use to establish sectional identities for themselves.

What God has done he has done; you can obscure it, or conceal it, or deny it, or renounce it. But you cannot put the clock back. You do indeed have the option of entangling yourselves in the mechanism of slavery, but this would be a matter of your deliberate will in turning your back on freedom. You cannot be both in and out of that mechanism. The slave style of life and the free style of life are irreconcilable. There is no co-existence in the end. In the first instance, the slave style will try to destroy the free. The free person presents an alarming threat to the child of slavery: the sectors of personality which want to be in bondage may well be far more energetic and aggressive than those which are willing to be liberated. But this is not the end of the story: the slave woman and her sons are to be cast out. You cannot attempt to 'find the good' in slavery, or preserve its best values. If the free way of being human is to be a genuine offer to man, it cannot be permanently compromised or diluted by a totally opposite principle.

Paul does not say, 'We are not children of *the* slave girl', but 'We are not children of *a* slave girl' – any slave girl. Paul won his particular battle: improbable though it may have seemed at the time, the church became an inclusive fellowship of Gentiles and Jews, and the enthusiasm for circumcision fell away. But there are many other forms of bondage in which the Christian community can be trapped, many other slave girls to adopt as mother. There are many other methods of organizing our acceptability by the maintenance of observable standards. We judge each other in accordance with the standards which happen to appeal to us. We search for a church which suits us, which will represent a god who suits us. The church which suits us will be the one which requires the least amount of change in us. This sort of religion seems to us to be 'good news'; it tells us that our acceptability is in our hands to create. It tells us that we must try harder at the things which come easiest, the things which we already recognize as being worth trying to do, for these are the things which have attracted us to our particular 'church'. In huge modern cities, one of the few ways in which people can feel significant is by belonging to highly specific religious groups, each defined by its difference from other groups. The one thing which these groups have in common is their habit of comparing themselves favourably with what they call 'most people'. They cultivate this minority character, and thus demonstrate that they are part of the slavery-system of exclusiveness.

Preserve Your Freedom 5:1–15

5:1 Paul is the apostle of freedom. He does not offer a theory of freedom; nor is he using his religious and political privileges in an attempt to appeal to the powerful to give a little more freedom to the powerless. Like Jesus before him, Paul moves among the powerless themselves. He bids the enslaved claim a freedom, he bids the disinherited claim an inheritance, which is already theirs.

Because of this strategy, Paul, like Jesus, was seen as a threat to security and became a victim of counter-revolutionary violence. It was because of this that he could claim to have been crucified. Paul and his message were successful, not through possessing the numerical or political power which could match violence with violence, but because the Christian community had a more effective set of symbols, a more powerful story than the myths and the symbols that inspired the communities of privilege. The Christian community could speak of and point to the cross and resurrection of Jesus. But Paul has to warn that we abandon this Christ, we lose our one and only security and claim, if we allow ourselves to get trapped in a new form of enslavement.

This has been the main danger for Christian faith ever since: it has been claimed by the power-bearers, and has been itself enslaved and distorted as a tool in the equipment of oppression. The fact that the power-bearers have thus trapped the Christian message is a witness that they have felt that the message is too dangerous to be allowed to move free and at large among the oppressed. But now, the intellectual, ideological, aesthetic and organizational controllers of our culture no longer reckon Christian gospel to be sufficiently important for them to bother about; they have become embarrassed by it. There is an ideological vacuum in the consciousness of the privileged, and the great traditional symbols of the gospel no longer are significant currency. This certainly seems to be true of metropolitan upper-class English culture – Culture with a big C. Consider, for instance, the extraordinary visual barrenness of the three high-prestige memorials recently erected by the power centre of English culture, at Runnymede – the Magna Carta Memorial, the John F. Kennedy Memorial, and the Air Forces Memorial. Those who have the power to design and commission such things appear to have lost all confidence in traditional symbols – indeed in iconography as a whole. Monuments of this kind testify to the expensive sense of duty, not to the liberated imagination, of those who are responsible for them. But, if this is a sign of the malaise of the privileged, it can be a sign of hope for our oppressed minorities and depressed majorities. The under-privileged have this choice before them: either they can pursue the privileged into the consumer ethic and the ideological vacuum; or they can hear and grasp and be motivated by the claim of the Jesus message, which tells them that there is a genuine freedom which is theirs already and that they therefore can avoid the trap of a new enslavement.

In quite specific ways, there is a parallel between the situation of Paul's hearers and the situation of all sorts of disadvantaged groups today, and some of them are claiming the kind of freedom which he was indicating to the Galatians. (For some of the most creative witness today, we look towards the areas of struggle in Latin America, in the work of people like Helder Camara, José Miguez-Bonino, Gonzalez Arroyo, Gustavo Guttierez, etc. And the Black South Africans who contribute to *Black Theology* [edited by Basil Moore] are working out new kinds of hope and critique which they do not owe to the white-based churches.) It is from groups like this that real renewal will be coming, not from the reforms which are being made within our wealthier churches; these churches will be watchers and gainers from other people's discovery of the freedom of the gospel.

Paul insists that his readers are free. He urges them, not to choose freedom, or to return to freedom, but to remain in freedom. Their freedom is not the freedom to choose between freedom and slavery. The freedom to choose is a bondage; you cannot move while you are undecided; you then have a freedom to dither and delay, which is nice for the privileged and sophisticated but is no use in face of the real bondages and crises. You find a truer freedom only after the choice is made, when you are committed to some person or some course of action.

But the freedom of which Paul speaks is neither the freedom of being able to choose, nor the freedom of having chosen. It is the freedom of having been chosen. It is the freedom of grace, the freedom of having been adopted and given freedom as children of God. It may look like bondage. But to live in order to acquire valuedness is bondage: to live with a given valuedness is freedom, for one's security is already established.

There is no purpose in being free. Paul says, 'For

freedom Christ has freed you' – not for any scheme or mechanism, not so that you can set up a whole lot of new goals and purposes. Those who are in bondage exist only to satisfy purposes. If there is to be freedom for them, it must come as a gift, not as part of a new system; otherwise, it is no different from their enslaved existence. In any situation of real bondage, there is no hope for freedom, if freedom is something to be organized or earned. This book is dedicated to those people, some of whom are very particular friends, who are under banning orders in South Africa. They have been deprived of most normal forms of freedom, but have been convicted of no crime. What do I say to a person in such a situation? Do I say, 'You are in bondage now, but you will be free in five years'? Do I say, 'You can choose, within the limits imposed on you, to be a free agent'? Surely I have to say to him, at the risk of sounding absurd or callous, 'My brother, you *are* free, your very situation testifies to the fact that you are free. Stand fast in the freedom with which Christ has set us free, for the children of bondage are doomed.'

The freed person will discover that free people are usually in the minority; this is why he needs to be urged to stand firm in his freedom. Once he starts expressing his freedom in any caring way, he will discover the boundaries. We can test the claim of a community to be freedom-loving by seeing the kind of people whom it restricts, and the kind of obstruction which they meet when they try to love their neighbours in any significant way. They will discover that the maintainers of bondage are in no uniform. A police state is not a state in which there are crowds of uniformed policemen in the streets: it is a state in which most members of the general public have allowed themselves to become unpaid and un-uniformed policemen.

2–4 Paul stresses again that to make an ambition of circumcision is incompatible with commitment to Christ. He is concerned with those who are positively seeking circumcision *now*, in the present tense. He is not condemning those who, by a cultural accident, have been circumcised long ago. To penalize those who were cir-

cumcised in this way would be to make Christ a slave of
uncircumcision: this is no better than making him the
slave of circumcision.

Paul's argument is not that the demands of the entire
law are loaded on to a misguided individual as an act of
arbitrary reprisal by an angry god. He is pointing out
the logic of the law itself, which is a complete system;
circumcision cannot be detached from it, for it has meaning only as a visible badge of a commitment to a vast
range of rituals and procedures. Those who are 'natural'
Jews can see the law as part of their ancient identity; it is
part of their subconscious, and can be a friend rather
than a burden. But those who deliberately become
circumcised will find themselves trapped in service of a
tyrant with insatiable demands. Once you start giving
power to this attitude of measuring people in terms of
qualifications you will find that you become enslaved to
it throughout your whole range of judgement and perception. The moment of becoming committed to this
way of being yourself is therefore absolutely critical. To
attempt to put oneself right with God by being good is to
reject the whole salvation brought by Christ.

5 We, by spirit, taking our faith as our point of departure, wait patiently for a hope of righteousness (the
literal meaning). Here is another contrast: the mind of
bondage identifies itself with what is, with what is identifiable and knowable. It has to find the evidence of
righteousness; it has to chalk up a score. The mind of
freedom can rest in hope. This is a powerful political
mandate. It involves both waiting for God's justice and
working to bring that justice into being. It involves
watching for signs of God's mind, and being sensitive to
God's activity. It means living with narrow horizons and
an invisible future.

This hope for righteousness includes a hope for
personal righteousness. The man of faith can live without
evidences of righteousness in himself; he can sit light to
his own emotional experience; he is not anxious about
whether he *feels* justified or accepted; he does not pursue
an experience of well-being for its own sake – he does not
use good behaviour as a kind of drug. He does not need

to have a score-card of perceived moral success. So, righteousness ought not to be seen as a qualification for membership of the community. Righteousness is something to be hoped for, rather than something to be claimed as a present achievement.

6 Paul stresses again that circumcision itself is not a bad thing but an indifferent thing; and the same is true of uncircumcision. He is not trying to increase the guilt of those who, through no choice of their own, happen to have been circumcised. But equally, he has no time for the 'more uncircumcised than thou' kind of approach.

'Circumcision' still has its disciples; there are legalism, sectionalism, racism, and there are people who delight in rules and rituals and religious insignia. There are others who delight in attacking all such things. 'Uncircumcision' prides itself on its freedom from religion and rules; there are groups which compete with each other to be most secular and to reject the largest number of conventions. In their search for this new kind of sectional security, they breed as much competitive anxiety and bondage to slogans as any 'conservative' body. Anarchism and counter-dependence are as enslaving and uncreative as conformism and over-dependence. Ideological circumcision and ideological uncircumcision both keep people in a state where they are prey for demogogues and rogues. They produce a followsheep of slaves rather than a fellowship of mature human beings.

7–8 What motivates people to reject the gracious offer and gift of freedom? What causes us to strive to put ourselves under authoritarian systems? It is one solution to the common human feeling of being alone and insignificant. To some people, freedom comes as freedom from support and security, and it is then a threat rather than a blessing. It becomes a burden which must be unloaded on to someone or something. Many people feel like this at a time of social, cultural or personal upheaval – the sort of condition which many of Paul's readers would have known. People in this kind of situation may well find themselves regressing into immaturity and striving to find a group to which to surrender their freedom.

It looks as though the Christians in Galatia had been caught in something like this state of mind, to judge both from Paul's analysis of their trouble and from his attempts to respond to it. Note that while he stresses the power of God's call to him, he carefully avoids any stress on the power or almightiness of Jesus Christ. He appears to be deliberately avoiding any argument which might lead his readers to surrender their personalities to a master-Christ – or even to a master-Paul. He chooses rather to stress ideas which would restore his readers' sense of personal significance – in the figure of the Son of God who loved me and gave his life for me.

Paul's readers are in danger of surrendering their minds and identities to an externalized system. That is a serious danger, and he is deeply disturbed by it. But there is a greater danger, and that would be to offer Christ himself as the one to whom the surrender must be made. The cure is not to find a better object for the surrender. Christ is the answer, not because he is the ideal tyrant but because he is the model of liberty. And his apostle has to strive to represent this model himself, in his efforts to persuade and to free the minds of his friends. So he stresses his confidence in them. In a situation of strain and fear, where people are setting up standards and spying on each other's loyalty and behaviour, it becomes difficult to trust others, because I know that I am not trusted myself. The remedy is not for me to struggle to intensify my faith. The remedy can come if someone else reliably and credibly convinces me that he has faith in me.

This is Paul's purpose here; and to make his words credible he stresses the fact that he distinguishes his readers from the person who has caused their trouble. He carefully avoids making the kind of comment which would merely intensify their sense of guilt.

9–10 'It takes only a little yeast to raise the whole batch of dough.' This could be a warning of the infectiveness of disorder. But it could also be an encouragement – 'It doesn't take much yeast to leaven all the dough. For myself, I believe that you have enough people with the right attitude among you, and this will spread among you all. But the man – he may be just a single individual – who is causing all this disturbance, he will carry the burden of judgement, whoever he is.' Paul is not necessarily referring to 'the punishment of God' – as a distinct act of punitive sentencing. He is saying that it is this stimulator of the disorder, rather than his misguided victims, who will find himself carrying the burden of scrutiny and evaluation. This reckoning of the use that he has made of his opportunities will weigh heavily on him. This is the warning which is properly set before anyone who teaches or influences other people's minds.

11 Paul is conscious that his record as a Pharisee is being used against him by ignorant or dishonest propagandists. 'These are his actual words,' they are saying, 'at a public meeting only twenty years ago!' Underneath it all, goes the accusation, he hasn't changed; he still preaches circumcision. Paul claims that this is nonsense. 'Once, indeed, I did preach a message commending circumcision, and won much approval. Then I started to preach the cross of Christ and was persecuted. But if, as my opponents allege, I am really still a preacher of circumcision, why do they continue to attack me? If I were still preaching circumcision, they would have no cause to call the cross a snare and a delusion' (literally, the trigger of a trap).

Paul does not claim that he is being persecuted for denouncing circumcision: such denunciaton is not his main aim in life. His primary commitment is the preaching of the cross, not an anti-circumcision polemic. A true representing of the meaning of Christ's death is likely to cause hostility and resentment, because it reduces the credibility and market value of the sectional or privileged kinds of security which all men treasure in their various groups.

12 But woe to the man who is causing the trouble! Such people are saboteurs against the city of God. The logical fulfilment for the apostles of circumcision would be to go the whole way and castrate themselves. The logical conclusion of an ideology of self-mutilation is that you bring about your own infertility.

For the Gentile Galatians, the distinctive mark of circumcision would have a value and attractiveness quite different from the value attached to it by the traditional Jew. For Jews, circumcision was the outward sign of a spiritual covenant, linked with a system of law which was ethically and intellectually demanding. For Gentiles, circumcision could easily have a much more shallow and dangerous meaning. Either it could be valued purely as an outward badge, as an observable way of becoming as respectable as Jews; or it could be a way of returning into the destructive rituals of paganism.

The gospel of Jesus Christ asserts the value of all of me. It does not require that anything be lopped off. Certainly it calls for purifying and dedication: it calls for sacrifice, of the kind represented by the cross. But this is a sacrifice of the whole self; it is not a way of achieving a state of grace by means of chopping off bits of myself. Castration, of one kind or another, has an immense appeal; it is an attack on a selected bit of oneself, to escape the judgement that is to be exercised on the whole self; or, it is an attempt to save the whole self by depriving oneself of a token bit of the whole self. Neither approach is compatible with the gospel of Jesus Christ.

13 Freedom is a call, a summons, a mandate. Freedom does not happen automatically: it happens because of God's deliberate intervention on behalf of the oppressed and enslaved. It is an act of creation, in which God pushes back the boundaries of chaos and darkness and calls light and order into being. The call of God raises Jesus from the dead, and makes Paul an apostle; the same call of God summons us into freedom. Our freedom, therefore, is something into which we move and grow. It is the freedom of maturity. The completely immature pianist is free to hit any note he likes: the completely mature pianist is free to play any piece of music he likes. Between these two kinds of freedom lies a period of discipline, training, rules, and traditions – the whole adolescence experience.

The irresponsible freedom of immaturity is not the freedom we are called into but the freedom we are growing from. This is the kind of distinction that Paul is making; he is anxious that his readers should not attach themselves to a sort of freedom which would be another kind of bondage. 'Freedom' is a dangerous idea when it gets into the hands of those who happen to be free to make slogans about freedom. All slogan-thinking ultimately serves the purposes of those who wish to keep the human spirit in slavery.

Paul is distinguishing between true freedom and the freedom claimed by those who live according to 'flesh'. The freedom to which we are called is not the freedom which many privileged people claim, the freedom to exploit other people, or the freedom to use wealth to get special advantage within the systems of law or education. This kind of freedom cloaks itself in such terms as 'enterprise' or 'initiative'; but, as Paul notes in verse 15, it becomes merely a freedom to destroy our fellow-men. Martin Luther had to make the same kind of distinction. Although the Reformation had indeed brought genuine liberation to many thousands, Luther was deeply distressed to see that some people immediately perverted the new freedom by claiming it as a freedom to do what they liked with their own property. They took it as a freedom to exploit, a freedom from the controls of conscience and law which previously would have restrained them from selling things for as much as they could get. For Luther, this was not freedom; it was 'flesh'. One of the most dangerous forms of 'flesh' was the unrestrained profit-motive (see his *Commentary*, p. 483). Paul and Luther are in fundamental conflict with the economic basis of our present civilization. Or what about our contemporary controversies concerning freedom of speech? In South Africa, the right to speak without political censorship has to be fought for and defended at great cost, and this has made me want to resist all attempts at banning, even when, as in the case of the National Union of Students, the intention is to ban people advocating fascism and racism. But the precious notion of 'freedom of speech' may itself be a deception. Freedom is falsely claimed unless it is being used in solidarity with the poor and in alliance with the unfree in their struggle. Freedom is falsely claimed unless it is participating in God's strategy of liberation. Christians have no mandate to stand up for the rights of those who, by word or action, seek to exploit their fellow-men.

This specific kind of problem is close to Paul's concern at this point. He therefore takes care to offer a guideline to help his readers to make the essential distinction. Genuine freedom is a freedom to be in solidarity with one's fellow-men; it is a freedom to love. It is not a new base-camp for the operations of the power that Paul calls 'flesh'. To live according to flesh is slavery; it is to let things happen according to the rule of the market; it is 'unredeemed' living; it is moral abdication; it is to rest in a definition of myself which alleges that I am *only* what the mechanisms have made me, that I am *only* the product of impersonal economic or social determinisms.

Fourteen times in *Galatians* Paul uses a word which is literally translated 'flesh'. The TEV avoids this literal translation; instead, it manages to find ten different expressions by which it attempts to convey the meaning of the word in various different contexts. Unfortunately, these are all misleading in one way or another. In the present context, for instance, we find the phrase 'physical desires'. But this is far too narrow an idea for representing the whole range of mental, imaginative, social and political motivations which Paul is concerned with. And so, when it comes to the list of 'works of flesh', the TEV switches to 'human nature'. But this implies that the nature of humanity is by definition hostile to the creator, which is certainly not part of Paul's argument. Elsewhere, the TEV uses the expressions 'your own power', 'natural desires', and 'external matters'. There is certainly a problem here, and most other modern translations in English wrestle with it with little success. The trouble about so many of these expressions like 'physical desires' and 'lower nature' is that they imply that the person can be divided off into sections; then I say that I 'have' these things, not that I 'am' them. I can dissociate from them and disclaim some of the responsibility; I can identify the disorder with a *bit* of me which has got out of control. Whether or not we find such an analysis helpful, it is not Paul's psychology. He chooses to use the word 'flesh', open as it is to serious misunderstanding, but works into it a whole range of meaning which cannot be contained within any of these alternative expressions. (He has added further difficulty by using the same word at 2:20 without any hostile overtones, to refer to ordinary human life within the ordinary world; 'in flesh', in this sense, he can live in faith and according to the mandates of spirit.) I believe that the older translations have the best solution. They share the problem with the reader. We take the word 'flesh', misleading as it is, but discover directly from the context the meaning that Paul is using it to convey. By 'flesh', he fundamentally means that whole bundle of powers that are hostile to freedom and to love. From his list of the activities of 'flesh', we can identify manifestations which could be called 'physical', while some are 'spiritual', some individual, some social. 'Flesh', therefore, is not a psychological term, but a behavioural or moral term. It is not a property or a possession of a person; it is an event, a way in which a person happens. 'Flesh' is not a deviant bit of me; it is me, the whole me – intellect, imagination, the lot – operating contrary to love and to spirit.

14 The law can be seen as a unity; it is all fulfilled in one activity, namely loving your neighbour as yourself. In such loving, each person recognizes and affirms both the other person's value and his own value. Where this is not happening, we pursue a value for ourselves, in separation from our neighbour; our search for status is a compensation for our own unlovedness. This is the specific danger of the Galatians' situation. You are loved, Paul is insisting, and this lovedness is the truest thing about you, just as it is the truest thing about me. The Son of God loved me and died for me. To refuse to love what God loves is to fly in the face of his will and of his generosity.

   This, Paul claims, is the true meaning and effect of the law of God. The God whom Jesus discloses is the God who makes this kind of law. In these terms, law is a powerful blessing to the world.

15 The opposite of this understanding of law is any system which makes people a prey. People become fuel

for other people's nourishment; people are used as
stepping-stones in ambitious pathways, or as victims in
competitive games. The uncircumcised is prey for the
circumcised, and vice versa. The whole Galatian situation
could be described as one of spiritual cannibalism. (The
TEV's phrase 'act *like animals*' is an unwarranted addition to the meaning of the Greek. Non-human animals
rarely 'destroy each other' *within their own species*.)
Paul points out that this cannibalism is incompatible,
not only with loving one's neighbour, but also with loving
oneself. This struggle to fatten oneself on the flesh of
others is self-destructive and is rooted in self-hatred. It is
based on the assumption that one has value only in
comparison with someone else's lack of value. In this
kind of struggle, the simple truth is that nobody can win.
We must either live together as brothers or die together
as fools.

The Spirit and the Flesh 5:16–26

[The TEV's heading for this section is 'The Spirit and
Human Nature', but I have preferred to use the more
literal term 'flesh', for reasons given on pp. 84–5.]

16–18 So Paul opens up the most specifically moral
section of the letter. But this is not a subject on its own:
it closely depends on all that has gone before. He dis-
cusses moral questions only after other grounds of
personal security are firmly established. Otherwise, to
raise comparisons of good and bad behaviour would
stimulate all the elements of self-justification and
competitiveness which are the most serious enemies of
gospel.

Paul does not merely say, 'Be good and stop being
bad' – the frustrating and infuriating message of moral
prophets (e.g. Isaiah 1:16–17). He contrasts spirit and
flesh, but even here he does not merely say 'obey the
spirit and not the flesh.' The TEV obscures the fact that
he offers one imperative only, the positive call to 'walk
by spirit'; the effect of this will be that 'you will not carry
out any desire of flesh.'

Life is a battleground between flesh and spirit. Because

of this opposition within your motivation, Paul says, you are frustrated, you cannot do what you wish to do. You fail to do the good things that you want to do. Equally, you fail to do the bad things you want to do. These people have so much conflict in their situation, that a great deal of their available energy is spent not in activity but in resistance to activity; they are free neither to be bad nor to be good. All possible courses of action have got something wrong or unattractive about them, and life is a long series of hang-ups. Now, Paul is writing very directly to these particular people. This is *your* experience, *your* condition, he claims. The Galatians are in the characteristic position of man under the law, of the depressed man who is frustrated by the bondage of conscience: the knowledge of good and evil is the inhibiting demand made by conscience that we have to give a 'good' or 'evil' label to every possibility. This demand can be the biggest obstacle to creative freedom, the most convenient device for those who wish to prevent change.

Those who are led by spirit are saved not only from flesh but also from law. Law does not save from flesh; it is flesh's ally. It operates in the same area and uses the same tools. Both seek to give us satisfaction and assurance in terms of our security in comparison with other people's insecurity; both claim to satisfy by being divisive, or by being mechanistic, automatic, impersonal, manipulative (the examples come in the next section). Law would seek to oppose flesh by building up an impressive set of claims or a weighty array of long-service-and-good-conduct awards. But this only exercises and emphasizes the same old trouble. The real opposite to evil is not virtue but spirit; and spirit, as we see later, does not have 'works' or 'activities' which can be quantified. It bears 'fruit' which is different in kind from the activities of flesh.

Spirit is opposite to flesh. It is the other way of being human. Spirit has already been described. Spirit is the spirit of God's Son, which gives us the voice and character of sons of God: and this spirit is shared among those who are prepared to see that the blessing of God is for all mankind.

Spirit is energy which enables man to claim, assert and live by a new kind of security, a security which depends on community and not on exclusiveness. By this spirit we can be led. In so far as we are led by spirit, or walk by spirit (Paul switches very easily from 'the spirit' to 'spirit'), we will not fulfil the desires of flesh and will also not be subject to law. We will be free. Thus the pattern of Paul's terminology is completed: spirit, faith and freedom are different aspects of a divine strategy, which is opposed to a hostile strategy characterized by flesh, law and slavery.

To walk by spirit does not mean that the flesh and its motivations are abolished. To the depressed or troubled conscience, this observation is not a further burden but a lifting of the gloom. The conflict which we experience is not a sign of our inexcusable badness; it is the common lot of the Christian disciple, and, in one sense, is nothing to worry about. The person who seriously cares about the way of the spirit will perceive all the more sharply the motivations and lures of the flesh. The Christian is not one who rests in his innocence, but is a genuinely creative person who pushes back the boundaries of the threatening chaos, who turns depression and failure into hope, who knows the secret whereby sin can be the precursor of a new righteousness, based on faith. Paul can look this conflict straight in the face, not because he stands clear in his own innocence, but because he knows himself to be forgiven. Where God is known to be forgiving, law loses its threat. Where God is known to be forgiving, the maintenance of human classifications on a moral basis becomes absurd: the past loses its power to decide who we are and where we must be. Where God is known to be forgiving, we can take the risk of walking by spirit.

19–21 The meaning of 'flesh' becomes more plain when we see the range of activities which Paul includes in his list of specimens. He includes, for instance, activities of sensual lust, represented by prostitution (his first item, exactly translated) and orgies. Sexual promiscuity is a retreat into a very private kind of behaviour; the sexual partner isn't around afterwards to enable the two-ness of the sex act to be worked out and implemented in inter-personal commitment. The exploitation of some-one else's body is valued self-satisfyingly, as a kind of pain-killing drug. So it is appropriate that the second item on Paul's list should be a term which implies a private, interior disorder. The third item is the opposite sort of evil, an unhelpful and cruel type of public dis-regard for people's sensitivities. In so far as these three items have sexual significance (and this is specific only in the first of them), it is essential to note that these are activities, not basic drives or powers. The whole tragedy of 'the flesh' is that it dehumanizes something which is human and corrupts that which is good. 'The flesh' causes a person to divert from the vocation of being human, by using sexuality as a form of flight from spirit, rather than as a form of involvement with spirit.

Then there is a group of activities of the flesh which are forms of political lust. These include all sorts of un-sanctified aggressiveness and competitiveness, the kind of ambition which cannot tolerate anyone else having any more than me, and the kind of ambition which insists that I must be one up on everyone else. These are social as well as individual disorders: they include the spreading of dissension and factionism, and the mercenary pur-chasing of people's loyalties for sectional groups. Playing power-games, whether in family, church or nation, is a flight from the calling of the spirit, into an intense con-cern about success and failure, a world where my place is determined by who is above me and who is below. But, as with sex, the thing in itself is good. Power is entrusted by God to the whole of mankind, as a hope and a blessing. But when power is used divisively and in exploitation, it becomes a main component in producing works of the flesh.

Paul also includes some activities which are forms of religious or intellectual lust, such as idolatry and witch-craft. Idolatry is essentially exclusive; its whole point is that my idol takes my side, and I hope that it is stronger than yours. It will serve my purposes, whether it is a fish-god or a highly sophisticated structure of speculation which can be approached only by those who have gone a long way through the filter-system of educational privilege. Witchcraft is a secret system whereby knowledge is reserved for a few and used by them to manipulate the fate of others. The competitiveness of much of our educational process encourages us to value knowledge as a private possession and make it public only when this will serve our private gain. Occultism and preoccupation with the supernatural, although they may speak of 'God' and the 'spiritual world', are manifestations of 'flesh'. They divert attention from the real battles of the spirit which have to be fought in the concrete situations of our search for the kingdom of God and his justice. The god who is implicated in idolatry and witchcraft is very far removed from the God who is known as Father. Devotion to such a god encourages us to believe that life is basically a matter of manipulation and clever tricks: those who wish to justify their manipulation of their fellow-men will devise a god who will fit in with the same principles.

The word translated 'witchcraft' means, more generally, 'dealing in drugs'. It can mean many different methods of evading the demands of the real world. Like the lust of sensuality and the lust of power, the lusts of religion and intellect are a flight from reality; but these lusts invite us to escape inwards instead of outwards, and to find a remedy for the anxieties of life in scoring intellectual or spiritual points and in 'being right'. This is yet another private or sectional pursuit; it reinforces my faith in my own performance. The gospel of Jesus Christ does not provide any escape-route from the pain and dread of the human condition: it offers no behavioural, social, political or religious anaesthetic. The gospel beckons man to move in another direction altogether. It calls us to identify with the Crucified, and to see the cross as the fundamental interpretation of life. The works of the flesh are either distractions, diversions, or means of withdrawal. The way of the cross is to face the conflict and agony head-on, in the company of one who has mastered them in his own experience. The lust for sensory satisfaction, the lust for power, and the lust for religious wizardry, were three options which Jesus rejected at the beginning of his ministry. He recognized them all as evasions of his calling, for all of them offered ways of avoiding the basic issues which were his to face as representative man. From then on, his face was set towards Jerusalem, the place of conflict, dread and death; the seductions of the flesh had no power to divert him from his life in the spirit as a son (Luke 4:1–13).

Paul ends this section with a forecast, that people who do the sort of things which he has described will not inherit the kingdom of God. The slave does not have any hope of inheritance, and the works of the flesh are the signs that people are keeping themselves in a slave state. To the extent that they keep themselves in a slave state, to that extent they are opting to stay under the law; and to that extent they are unable to share in the inheritance. This is not a punishment for making the wrong choice; it is part of the choice itself.

The phrase 'the kingdom of God' is rare in Paul's writings. In over half of the occasions when the phrase occurs in writings attributed to him, he is making a negative statement that someone or other cannot or will not inherit the kingdom of God. Elsewhere Paul is very positive about the idea of 'inheritance'; but this is when he speaks of sharing in the inheritance of Abraham, or of Christ as Son of God. This suggests that the concept of 'inheriting *the kingdom of God*' was not one which Paul found helpful: he seems to be concerned to warn people who had assumptions about 'inheriting the kingdom of God' that they should think again. It looks as though the whole concept had become casual jargon among his readers. When a concept like 'kingdom' becomes jargon, it can easily be used to support just those assumptions of authoritarianism and group superiority which Paul found most threatening to the gospel. 'Kingdom' is a dangerous idea in the minds of people who are not committed to Christ's kind of kingship.

22–23 Of the flesh, there are works; it is possible to suggest a wide variety of specimens, and their identity is obvious; they are activities which can be observed and specified. Paul does not give us a corresponding list of 'works' of the spirit. He does not offer a programme of cultivating certain virtues as remedies for certain vices, or a seven-a-side morality as a check-list for our performance. He is not urging us to *do* anything. The spirit produces 'fruit'. Fruit comes by the slow and hidden process of growth, through infancy through adolescence to maturity. There are flowers on the way, no doubt, in the form of attractive and helpful activities; but the real signs of spirit are mature attitudes and directions of life.

Paul's imagery has its limitations. Language of 'fruit', 'growth', 'adolescence' and 'maturity' obviously has something to do with age. But this is not to say that the fruit of the spirit is limited to the over-forties. The kind of maturity which Paul refers to has practically no correlation with physical age. His list of 'works of the flesh' includes old men's sins. In any case, the main feature of Paul's religion, among its contemporaries, was that it was a *new* way, a young movement, attacking the calculating morality, the exclusivist dependence on ancestry, and the cynical rationalism bred from old laws, old identities and old gods. Paul was offering wisdom and maturity in the voice and vesture of a cocky young upstart.

Forbearance, for instance (the fourth in Paul's list), is a gift of maturity; it means rejecting the weapons which my enemy puts into my hand, and refusing to be infected by his hostility. It is the very secret of non-violence. This requires a good deal of skill in coping with my anxieties and my vulnerability. But the old are not necessarily more forbearing than the young: those who are furthest from forbearance are those who have the longest history of implementing the lusts of power.

Humility is another type of fruit. Humility happens when I stop valuing myself in terms of the privileges which distinguish me from other people. It happens when I realize more of the real range of my worth, when I realize that my value depends on my involvement with other people and not on the things that I can select and organize on my own. Only through humility of this kind can the more privileged person be free to identify with the oppressed and poor, to share their situation, their pain and their struggle: otherwise his intervention is another kind of boasting or imperialism. Humility is equally necessary for the oppressed themselves, for their condition does not guarantee humility: for them, humility means they do not fight to acquire value for themselves; they fight in confidence in a value which they have already as human beings. Humility of this kind will enable them to continue in the fight for justice wherever it leads them; thus they fight without losing their integrity – which is perhaps the best translation of Paul's sixth term.

Paul's final example of fruit is 'self-control'. This is the opposite of being controlled by someone else, which is slavery. It includes the courage and wisdom to make my own judgements, neither in infantile enslavement to authority nor in adolescent rejection of authority: the maturity to take responsibility for my own belief and conscience, and not to hand over such responsibility to any political or religious or cultural authority: the ability to hear and care for the other person without being dominated by my own anxieties: a care for the wholeness and usefulness of my reason and my central nervous system and the whole bundle of faculties by which people can help each other – if I hand over my autonomy to prejudices or drugs I am simply less available for other people: a consciousness of where my basic commitments lie, for these enable and nourish my freedom to love other people appropriately, responsibly and reliably. In short, this fruit of the spirit is a gift of self-government, autonomy, independence.

Against the fruit of the spirit, law is powerless and irrelevant. The fruit of the spirit cannot be prevented by law, nor can it be enforced by law. The works of the flesh can be assessed in legal terms, but the fruit of the spirit cannot be. The most that law can do for the good man is to permit him to be; it cannot regulate his nature. *For* spirit, it has only a slight role: *against* spirit, it has no role at all.

24–25 The flesh is doomed; those who belong to Christ Jesus have crucified the flesh, with its goals and ambitions. The TEV translation is misleading in two ways here. Firstly, Christians are not in conflict with their own individual 'flesh' only; the conflict against flesh is against the whole conspiracy of evil, public and institutional as well as private and internal. Secondly, Paul claims that

Christians have *crucified* the flesh, not necessarily that
they have already succeeded in completely killing it off.
Crucifixion was more than just a method of killing; it
was also a way of exposing people to public contempt:
it was like a very severe form of being put in the stocks
or pillory. It was a kind of killing, certainly, but a very
protracted kind of killing. It was a way of living as well
as a way of dying. The victim could hang on his cross
for days, and would eventually die of exhaustion and
starvation rather than from actual injury. Hardly anyone
would notice the moment of death, and the corpse was
normally left to rot and disintegrate slowly. This was
normal crucifixion, the meaning of the word in ordinary
conversation. When Paul speaks of crucifying the *flesh*,
he cannot be thinking of all the traditional Christian
implications of crucifixion, such as the suffering of the
innocent. He must be thinking much more simply of
crucifixion as the recognized method, throughout the
Roman Empire, of getting rid of dangerous and criminal
elements. His meaning could be expanded thus: There *is*
a conflict going on; there's no point in pretending
otherwise. If the flesh were not a reality to us still, there
would be no need to go into all this detail about it. Yes,
but you have already put it more where it belongs. Its
hands and feet are tied and nailed, and its criminal
character is exposed for all to see. It is screaming and
struggling and appealing for sympathy; but, with all its
weaknesses, sensitivities and vulnerability (this is what
the word 'passions' is about), along with its lusts and
demands and ambitions, it is doomed. For all its noise
and claim, it is not going to live, and cannot give us life.
Our true life is from the spirit.

26 Paul now returns right back to the immediate situation, to the point from which he began his discussion of
flesh and spirit in verse 15. In the light of all that is most
deeply true about us, he says, the Galatians must not
start to make stupid boasts, or to pitch rival claims at
each other, or to breed resentment. The TEV translation
of verse 26 is too generalized: Paul is specifically accusing
his readers of an actual and deplorable change of behaviour. They are becoming vainglorious, and attaching

value to insignificant distinctions between themselves; and this is threatening to produce competitiveness and a bandying about of challenges; and this in turn will lead these people into the whole destructive complex of status-anxiety called envy. This whole process is a reversion to life according to the flesh.

Bear One Another's Burdens 6:1–10

1–5 This follows straight on from the previous section. Competitiveness and envy thrive on the discovery of other people's points of weakness. Man under law, man according to the flesh, rejoices to discover what is wrong in others, because this enables him to allay his own anxieties. For the man suffering from anxiety about his status and his acceptability, bad news becomes good news, and the idea that there can be an intervention which would reduce this badness is most unwelcome. The worst news would be that there will be no more bad news. Where there is no bad news, the media perish.

It is precisely in such circumstances that the test comes, which indicates whether we are led by the spirit or not. Humility, as we have seen, is part of the fruit of spirit; and Paul here applies the term 'humility' to a specific situation (although the TEV translation does not indicate this). 'Brothers', he calls them, reminding them emphatically that this is what they have become. 'Brothers, suppose someone is caught in the act of some kind of lapse from right conduct; then you who are of spirit act in a spirit of humility: you repair that man (as if he were a broken bone).' He adds a warning that there is nothing exceptionally wrong with the man who happens to get caught flagrantly in the act: the helper and the helped belong in the same community.

At this deceptively simple point, we meet one of the sharpest forms of disorder in the Christian community, a point at which the whole proclamation of *Galatians* is a continual criticism of our fellowship. For it is one of the most universal characteristics of the church, bridging all the divisions of denomination and confession, that its keenest adherents tend to establish their power by fear and by the threat of rejection. This censoriousness is surely the worst single disease of the church, far more dangerous than its structural fragmentation, far more unconscious than its more obviously moral failures. It is to be found among 'radicals' not less than among 'conservatives'. Those who claim to be permissive seem often to be no more tolerant than their opponents; they have merely chosen different targets. And all this comes because our interest in being good is greater than our interest in God himself.

Brothers, people who together live by spirit, will be mindful of what unites them, and this will be more important than what separates them. This is not just a matter of differences of wealth or race or age or education: it applies to the most serious difference of all, the moral difference. The moral offender, particularly the one who is notoriously caught in the act, betrays the rest of the brotherhood, and the pressure to disown him is immense. This is particularly true where the brotherhood is an unpopular minority, and the offender has given way to the temptation to conform to public opinion. The best that man under the law can do is to respond, 'There, but for the grace of God, go I.' But this is a low estimate of the grace of God, if all that grace can do is to save us from conspicuous offence. Paul is asking his readers to look at the offender and say, 'There, *because* of the grace of God, *am I*.' That is my brother, and I treat his burden as my own; I live in his body, in his skin, in his shoes. This involves appearing to condone evil, to become identified with the other person's guilt and to abandon the standards by which life is best regulated. But it is part of fulfilling the law of Christ, the law of love. For we have to love people as they are, not as we would design them. We have to love the real church which is, and not a dream which is not. Anyone who wants to put things right in church or society has to ensure that he is not more in love with his dream than with the real people he professes to care for. This calls for self-control, a disciplining of the imagination. Make a realistic evaluation of your role and your work, Paul urges, and do not rely on public opinion. Other people may compare you with your fellows, either to your credit or to your discredit. But it doesn't really matter whether you are more conscientious than Mrs A or whether you are a worse organizer than your predecessor. If you evaluate yourself in these terms, you are mentally enslaving Mrs A or your predecessor to take responsibility for the way in which you are evaluated: you are making them carry a load which is yours and yours alone. Your evaluation, therefore, must be independent; avoid comparisons with other people, even in the process of devising the terms in which to do the evaluation. The only comparison that is valid is the comparison between the you that is and the you that you could be, the comparison between the actual and the potential. But this is not just a matter of negative self-accusation, although that may come into it. Primarily, it is your basic source of encouragement; it is a perception of God's design working out in you, a disclosure of where you are beginning to go, or to grow, or to glow.

We are to carry the burdens of each other: each person must carry his own load. The translation correctly represents a distinction in the original. The 'burden' is sheer heavy weight. It is the moral dead-weight of living in terms of law, and the spiritual dead-weight of unresolved guilt. The 'load' is something quite different: this is the duty that any responsible person is expected to accept: it is the freight which a ship is designed to carry and without which it bobs about uncontrollably on the water. To love means to carry one another's *burdens*: to love means also to let the other person carry his own proper *load*.

To be able to discern between burdens and loads, the helper has to be able to perceive beyond the signals fed to him by his own anxieties: our anxieties about our own time and resources prevent us from being available for carrying other people's burdens. Equally, our anxiety to prove our commitment, or to keep ourselves in business, or to avoid silence, can make us insist on interfering with other people's responsibility for carrying their own loads. We barge in full of covert self-regard; paternalistically or patronizingly or pauperizingly or proprietorially, we insult blacks and adolescents by excusing them from responsibility for their mistakes or by trying to ensure that they will never have to take responsibility for anything.

6 Now follows a blatantly domestic instance of the right handling of these responsibilities. The TEV translation of verse 6 is as satisfactory as can be got, but English cannot reproduce the heavy stress on the verb 'share' in the original. The phrase 'the man who is being taught' represents a word which transliterates directly into the word 'catechumen'. The catechumen – the pupil under instruction for baptism – enters into a brotherly relationship with his teacher, and is urged to 'communize' with his catechist in all good things. He has to see his teacher as a brother whose burdens he can share and whose needs he can make his own. By doing so, he is taking his place in the community which holds good things in common; he is becoming a partner with his teacher and with the rest of the community. Paul's word here is an instruction to the 'catechumen' to do this; equally, it is an instruction to the community to enable him to do so, and not to keep him out until he has earned his way in.

The catechumen is being brought into a community of sharing in which there is no such thing as *private* property or *private* power. Also, within Christian community, no one should be only a recipient. The point is not that people should be forced to earn their instruction, or their membership of the community; but, from the start, new members should be seen as people with a stake in the whole enterprise. They are not in a separate, irresponsible category merely because they are under instruction.

Paul is speaking of 'the person who instructs'. He is concerned about a person who fulfils a specific task, not one who happens to have a special status. He is anxious not to maintain ministers of religion as such but to ensure that education does not go by default. The church needs to ensure that its educators have the time and the freedom to enable them to work properly. If we took Paul's word seriously, local churches would be spending more on their education work than they do, for instance, on their music; a person who teaches children or helps a youth group would receive at least the kind of honorarium that would reduce his need to work overtime on his ordinary job, and would encourage him to equip himself for his teaching work; and the council would assume that books and equipment and training courses should have very high priority on its budget.

7–8 In the security of the gospel, we have a mandate to take responsibility for our future. We can sow seed into our flesh-system (this time, the TEV translates 'flesh' as 'natural desires'), and get a harvest of corruption – not just of 'death'. We can make ourselves allies of the old, destructive, exploitive, competitive style that is character-ized as 'flesh', and we can perpetuate its area of repro-duction. Or we can 'sow into the spirit', and from the spirit reap a wealth of fellowship, trust and commitment that is stronger than all the forces of destruction. This is 'life-eternal', a gift of grace, a fruit of spirit, known and shared now amid the general confusion and mess of our present experience.

Every contribution to truth and justice is a working-out of this mandate to sow into the spirit. There is a harvest; the sowing is worthwhile. The cults of anarchy, nihilism, despair and pessimism are ultimately irrespon-sible. Indeed, although they emerge as critiques of the *status quo*, they are fundamentally reactionary, for they resign all initiatives into the hands of those who use power to exploit their fellow-men. They are another device of the powers of darkness. The cosmos is not ultimately absurd: God is not the victim of a great joke, and his children can be assured that their commitment to his truth and justice is not a waste. But results do not come immediately; the harvest cannot be hastened arti-ficially. Our task now is not to worry and speculate overmuch about the future, but to make the most of the present opportunities for doing good.

9 Much of Paul's thought is subtle, and much of it seems to call for a lot of exploration and reflection. But there is no escaping this simple reminder that our task is to do good. This, in a vitally important sense, is what the Christian mission is all about; and I wonder very much whether time spent on books like this would not have better been spent on some more obvious way of 'doing good'. I leave this matter without comment, therefore, as

comment would be a misrepresentation of this clear mandate.

10 There is, however, Paul's extra phrase. Why must we do good *especially* to the family of faith? This looks like the old exclusiveness coming in by the back door. But this whole section, from the end of chapter 5, has been properly concerned with the internal life of the Christian community. The Christian mission is not just a way of universal benevolence: it is a new community based on a family relationship with God through his Son. To be of faith is to live by the vision of the inclusive purpose of God for all people. So a group which knows itself as the family of faith must have a wide responsibility outside itself, but precisely for this reason it has a responsibility towards itself as well. It has a mandate to care about the whole world; this is its task-responsibility. It also has a mandate to care about itself; this is its maintenance-responsibility. If it is careless about its domestic life, it is not likely to be of much use to the rest of the world.

Final Warning and Greeting 6:11-18

11 Paul ends this unusually personal letter with an unusually long personal conclusion. He begins by drawing attention to the fact that the pen is now in his own hand. This is no secretary or intermediary who is addressing you: it is me, myself. My secretary is professionally neat and orderly, economical in the use of ink and paper. That is the secretary's competence. But at this point I am taking over, for economy and neatness are no longer the most urgent needs; at this point, I want you really to pay attention, even if all the preceding paragraphs have passed over you.

12-13 Firstly, Paul says, don't be tricked by all this commendation of circumcision. There are people who want only to present a good image in terms of flesh: it is people like that who are trying to force circumcision on you. They want you to be circumcised so that they can use what happens in your flesh as the ground for their own claim for approval.

Paul uses once again this word 'flesh'. Although the word obviously does have a bodily reference here, we cannot forget the whole range of demonic meaning which Paul has previously worked into it; 'external matters' is too neutral a translation. These people want to feel that they have pulled you into the whole disorder that is meant by 'flesh'; they want to trap you in a world of legalism, where people are valued in terms of outward image and performance. And this is because they are afraid that, if they cannot credibly claim to be identified as agents of circumcision, they will be identified as agents of the cross of Christ and be persecuted.

For these people who are being circumcised do not cherish the law (note that Paul is not attacking all people who *have been* circumcised, who would include faithful Christian Jews). They do not value law as the revealing of the will of God but as a means of establishing a special kind of security for themselves. The very fact that they are prostituting the rite of circumcision like this shows that they do not really value the principle of law. True law is not intended to provide devices to enable one group to achieve its goals by manipulating another group.

Paul is here condemning any kind of using of people to substantiate our claim before God. We cannot use our list of converts or the receivers of our charity as a claim for approval or acceptance. They have every right to refuse to be used as a means by which we can achieve our own salvation. We may not use our work for people as a way of avoiding the real demand to be identified with the cross. The cross, in human terms, is a sign of failure, not of success, and it is the only ground of our claim. We put our trust not in what we have succeeded in getting other people to do but in what Christ has done for us.

14 This kind of destructive and parasitic ideology produces so much 'boasting' – so much mindless fervour – that many of us become sceptical about all enthusiasm. The terrible examples, in this century, of racialist ideology have made a lot of people hope for a cool value-free world of objectivity. But this is an illusion of the intellectually privileged; it is in effect a permission to false enthusiasms to propagate themselves without hindrance.

The under-privileged know perfectly well that a dispassionate concern for objectivity is a poor substitute for a passionate concern for liberation. Paul's answer to the cannibalistic boasting of his opponents is not a cool neutralism; he has his own boast, a valid boast, a boast that summarizes his enthusiasm for the integrity of all mankind; he makes his boast in the cross of Christ.

Paul has earlier stated that he has been crucified. He has also stated that flesh has been crucified. Now he links these together. The cross of Christ is the instrument by which both I and world are crucified to each other ('world' here seems to mean the same as flesh, but flesh operating on a universal scale). I look at world, and to me it is doomed; it is nailed up and its power is finished. World looks at me and sees me as a criminal crucified as Jesus was, and having no other claim. From now on, world and I have nothing to do with each other. I can accept the fact that world considers me a reject, for my rejection is the same as that of Christ: and I can reject world's rejection of me, because world is doomed.

15 Because world is doomed, all the distinctions that it cherishes are doomed also. Of these, the distinction between circumcision and uncircumcision is the most immediate and the most representative. As Paul has said before, the point is not that circumcision is the villain, but that neither matters any longer. Those who claim that the hope for humanity is in submission to an authority are hoping in vain. The hope of getting everyone circumcised is not hope at all, but a disguise for a real hopelessness. The law is a device to avoid the real dread. The ideology of circumcision is an anaesthetic.

But so is the ideology of uncircumcision. There are those who, far from opposing one law with another, reject the whole idea of law altogether. They maintain that there is no valid meaning in such ideas as conscience, morality and guilt. To the conscientious religious person, there seems to be an inexplicable alliance between the highly sophisticated anarchist intellectual and the semi-literate anti-social hooligan who lives only for the pleasure of the moment. Given sufficient stimulus from the advocates of 'circumcision', the intellectuals and the hooligans can form a powerful alliance to stand for their inalienable right to be uncircumcised. They form a party together to join combat with the circumcision party. But the uncircumcision party becomes as shrill, irrational and slogan-ridden as the circumcision party, and the circumcision party becomes as devious and as indifferent to truth as the uncircumcision party. The two parties are really on the same wavelength, like the prisoner who unconsciously walks in step with his escort.

Paul claims that neither of these two busily articulate positions copes with the real situation at all. They both depend on the continuing existence of each other, and of the evil and fear which they identify in each other; otherwise, they would both go out of business.

But what if something new breaks in which makes these commitments unnecessary? And how does one identify this new creation? It will be as subversive of ordinary subversion as ordinary subversion is subversive of law; it will be different in kind. It will baffle and elude the Security Police – the political, cultural and religious enforcers of conformity which all systems set up in one way or another. The Security Police will not know what to look for, for it will not have the usual array of manifestos, dogmas and programmes which they are trained to detect. Those who are infected by new creation will recognize each other, but not by any code that can be cracked by security. They will recognize each other, according to circumstances, by silence, a wink, an act of caring or of weeping, by a laugh or by a refusal to take something seriously. They will seem to be threatening, mad, or pointless to those who identify only with the old order.

According to the scriptures, the first creation did not just happen, out of nothing: creation happened out of chaos. It is not just an emanation or an evolution but a victory. And the same is true of new creation. It does not take place in the temple or the desert or the quiet hillside, or in the place of human success. The cross is the sign of new creation; new creation takes place at the centre of the storm, where the best law and religion of the world have proved ineffectual against injustice and prejudice, where men have turned their backs on freedom

and have become irrational slogan-shouters, and where
truth is treated as an expendable luxury. It is out of this
chaos and this dying that new creation comes. It is towards the areas of chaos rather than towards the areas
of success that we should look to see new creation today.
In such a situation, agents of new creation develop a new
kind of skill, not the skill to deflect chaos by trying to
identify who is to blame, but the skill somehow to live
through chaos and to discover new creation in it. This is
not so rare an experience as it may sound. Many people
get a taste of it in coping with personal tragedies of
various kinds. Corporately, this kind of renewal appears
as the deepest hope in such situations of chaos as Northern Ireland. There comes a time when the people who
have the power to pass important resolutions, or to write
impressive editorials, just run out of words. There is
nothing more that the liberal conscience from outside
can say. But new creation happens, among people who
do not have this armament of words. It can be seen when
people discover that they are more than their traditional
identities would allow them to be. They start taking
responsibility for what they really are, instead of letting
some circumcision group or uncircumcision group decide
everything for them. This makes the politicians seem
relatively unimportant, and it therefore misses the attention of the mass media. I cannot be more specific, but
anyone who has close Christian friends in Northern
Ireland will know what I'm referring to. It is an experience of creativity in chaos; it is denied to those who
commit themselves to a form of circumcision or uncircumcision, for they keep themselves clear of the real
places of dread.

16 The gospel of Jesus Christ is the most complete
authentic model by which to interpret our own experience
of chaos. This is what ordinary simple Christian discipleship is about, and it is important not to wrap it up in so
much fancy language that it is outside our range when
we most need it. This is a line, a direction of life, Paul
says, according to which we can order our steps. For
those who do so, there is a blessing of peace and mercy.
And from them, this blessing spreads to all the people

whom God is making his Israel, all the children of Abraham.

17 This basic peace Paul now claims for himself. Deep down he has an assurance and security which no complaint or criticism can touch. He belongs to the one who loves him, in a way that is not irrational but is in a legitimate sense beyond question. He is because he is loved, not because he is circumcised or uncircumcised, not because he deserves it or has earned it, not because he has passed any examination. This again is what simple Christian piety is all about, and it makes sense to anyone who knows, even on a limited scale, how the experience of being loved nourishes an unassailable security in the core of one's being. With this kind of security a person can venture into the most complete insecurity and live without landmarks and without special identity.

So, says Paul, let no one harass me or disturb me; for I carry on my body the marks of Jesus. All the previous argument has taken place because people want to get the signs that they belong to a particular religious and cultural group. But there is no security to be found in this; it merely produces groups and counter-groups, ideologies and counter-ideologies. But something new has come, which puts these groups and ideologies into the past and makes them irrelevant; this new thing is the cross of Christ, the Christ in whom there is neither circumcised nor uncircumcised, the Christ in whom there is neither Jew nor Gentile nor any other distinction, the Christ who loved me and died for me. This gives me a security which no longer depends on my being separate from anybody, for this security is for all the children of Abraham, for all mankind. I belong to this Christ, and the only marks that I am concerned about are the marks which show that I belong to him.

It is not necessary to pin down the exact meaning of these 'marks'. Paul does not identify himself, as the TEV translation insists, as a *slave* of Jesus. (The 'marks' – 'stigmata' – were marks made by branding, but slaves were not the only people who carried such marks in Paul's day, and he does not specify his meaning precisely. If he had really intended to identify himself, after all, as a *slave*, he would have surely made this clear.) All that Paul claims is that the marks that he carries are the marks of Jesus. Other marks, which may indicate membership of one or other group of people, are of no interest any longer. The marks of Jesus cannot be set up as a new kind of physical badge, to decide who is in and who is out. But the marks of Jesus are not just a vague image of goodwill. Although Paul does not specify this in so many words, we cannot ignore the one definite instance known to us of the marks of Jesus, namely the marks of crucifixion which remain irremovable evidence of the damage done to his human body by the crucifixion process. These marks assure us that Jesus was hurt as men are hurt; he was not just God in disguise. If Jesus had been able to survive crucifixion unscathed, this would not be a saving miracle; it would have been a dramatic demonstration of divine superiority, which would have merely emphasized the ancient divide between God and man. The marks of Jesus show that this most fundamental apartheid and division have been overcome; they show that there has been a real miracle, one that men can share. The marks of Jesus show that there has been a genuine victory over death, over all that separates man from man, over all the destructiveness of law and flesh and enslavement. The marks of Jesus show that this victory is given to man. They show that it is worthwhile standing for truth in the face of prejudice and compromise. They show that it is worthwhile claiming freedom in an enslaving world.

Paul claims that the marks of Jesus are on his own body. The power and effect of Jesus' victory are not reserved to Jesus so that we can worship him from a distance, but are shared with his people so that we can follow him and belong in his family.

18 So Paul ends by claiming this blessing for his readers also. These unfortunate, confused and anxious people whom he has rebuked and cajoled and lectured, they also share in this grace, the powerful, joyful initiative of Jesus Christ, who is Lord for all of us. As is his custom, Paul puts no verb into his final sentence. It is a prayer, that grace may be with them. It is also an affirmation, that grace is with them. In present and in future, the grace of our Lord Jesus Christ remains the deepest truth about them.

There remains the next-to-last word. This 'brothers' really is unusual. No other letter in the New Testament ends like this, with a word of address in such a strange and emphatic position. 'Brothers' is Paul's final statement. The translation *'my* brothers' is an interpretation which is not required by the original text. Paul simply addresses his readers as 'Brothers'. Certainly, they are his brothers, but equally they are brothers of each other, they are brothers within the whole family and household of faith, sharers in the inheritance, sons alongside the Son of God. For us, too, they are brothers, brothers in the battle against sin and enslavement. This 'brothers' is us. This 'brothers' is the summary of the whole battle, the whole document. This is the gospel of Jesus Christ.

The last word. Amen. Yes, Lord, yes indeed.

PAUL'S LETTER TO THE GALATIANS

1 From Paul, whose call to be an apostle did not come from man or by means of man, but from Jesus Christ and God the Father, who raised him from death. ²All the brothers who are here join me in sending greetings to the churches of Galatia:

³May God our Father and the Lord Jesus Christ give you grace and peace.

⁴In order to set us free from this present evil age, Christ gave himself for our sins, in obedience to the will of our God and Father. ⁵To God be the glory forever and ever! Amen.

The One Gospel

⁶I am surprised at you! In no time at all you are deserting the one who called you by the grace of Christ, and are going to another gospel. ⁷Actually, there is no "other gospel," but I say it because there are some people who are upsetting you and trying to change the gospel of Christ. ⁸But even if we, or an angel from heaven, should preach to you a gospel that is different from the one we preached to you, may he be condemned to hell! ⁹We have said it before, and now I say it again: if anyone preaches to you a gospel that is different from the one you accepted, may he be condemned to hell!

¹⁰Does this sound as if I am trying to win men's approval? No! I want God's approval! Am I trying to be popular with men? If I were still trying to do so, I would not be a servant of Christ.

How Paul Became an Apostle

¹¹Let me tell you, my brothers, that the gospel I preach was not made by man. ¹²I did not receive it from any man, nor did anyone teach it to me. Instead, it was Jesus Christ himself who revealed it to me.

¹³You have been told of the way I used to live when I was devoted to the Jewish religion, how I persecuted without mercy the church of God and did my best to destroy it. ¹⁴I was ahead of most fellow Jews of my age

in my practice of the Jewish religion. I was much more devoted to the traditions of our ancestors.

[15]But God, in his grace, chose me even before I was born, and called me to serve him. And when he decided [16]to reveal his Son to me, so that I might preach the Good News about him to the Gentiles, I did not go to anyone for advice, [17]nor did I go to Jerusalem to see those who were apostles before me. Instead, I went at once to Arabia, and then I returned to Damascus. [18]It was three years later that I went to Jerusalem to get information from Peter, and I stayed with him for two weeks. [19]I did not see any other apostle except James, the Lord's brother.

[20]What I write is true. I am not lying, so help me God! [21]Afterwards I went to places in Syria and Cilicia. [22]At that time the members of the Christian churches in Judea did not know me personally. [23]They knew only what others said, "The man who used to persecute us is now preaching the faith that he once tried to destroy!" [24]And so they praised God because of me.

Paul and the Other Apostles

2 Fourteen years later I went back to Jerusalem with Barnabas; I also took Titus along with me. [2]I went because God revealed to me that I should go. In a private meeting with the leaders, I explained to them the gospel message that I preach to the Gentiles. I did not want my work in the past or in the present to go for nothing. [3]My companion Titus, even though he is Greek, was not forced to be circumcised, [4]although some men, who had pretended to be brothers and joined the group, wanted to circumcise him. These people had slipped in as spies, to find out about the freedom we have through our union with Christ Jesus. They wanted to make slaves of us. [5]We did not give in to them for a minute, in order to keep the truth of the gospel safe for you.

[6]But those who seemed to be the leaders—I say this because it makes no difference to me what they were; God does not judge by outward appearances—those leaders, I say, made no new suggestions to me. [7]On the contrary, they saw that God had given me the task of

preaching the gospel to the Gentiles, just as he had given Peter the task of preaching the gospel to the Jews. [8]For by God's power I was made an apostle to the Gentiles, just as Peter was made an apostle to the Jews. [9]James, Peter, and John, who seemed to be the leaders, recognized that God had given me this special task; so they shook hands with Barnabas and me. As partners we all agreed that we would work among the Gentiles and they among the Jews. [10]All they asked was that we should remember the needy in their group, the very thing I have worked hard to do.

Paul Rebukes Peter at Antioch

[11]When Peter came to Antioch, I opposed him in public, because he was clearly wrong. [12]Before some men who had been sent by James arrived there, Peter had been eating with the Gentile brothers. But after these men arrived, he drew back and would not eat with them, because he was afraid of those who were in favour of circumcising the Gentiles. [13]The other Jewish brothers started acting like cowards, along with Peter; and even Barnabas was swept along by their cowardly action. [14]When I saw that they were not walking a straight path in line with the truth of the gospel, I said to Peter, in front of them all, "You are a Jew, yet you have been living like a Gentile, not like a Jew. How, then, can you try to force Gentiles to live like Jews?"

Jews and Gentiles Are Saved by Faith

[15]Indeed, we are Jews by birth, and not Gentile sinners. [16]Yet we know that a man is put right with God only through faith in Jesus Christ, never by doing what the Law requires. We, too, have believed in Christ Jesus in order to be put right with God through our faith in Christ, and not by doing what the Law requires. For no man is put right with God by doing what the Law requires. [17]If, then, as we try to be put right with God by our union with Christ, it is found that we are sinners as much as the Gentiles are—does this mean that Christ has served the interests of sin? By no means! [18]If I start to build up again what I have torn down, it proves that I am breaking the Law. [19]So far as the Law is concerned, however, I am dead—killed by the Law itself—in order

that I might live for God. I have been put to death with Christ on his cross, [20]so that it is no longer I who live, but it is Christ who lives in me. This life that I live now, I live by faith in the Son of God, who loved me and gave his life for me. [21]I do not reject the grace of God. If a man is put right with God through the Law, it means that Christ died for nothing!

Law or Faith

3 You foolish Galatians! Who put a spell on you? Right before your eyes you had a plain description of the death of Jesus Christ on the cross! [2]Tell me just this one thing: did you receive God's Spirit by doing what the Law requires, or by hearing and believing the gospel? [3]How can you be so foolish! You began by God's Spirit; do you now want to finish by your own power? [4]Did all your experience mean nothing at all? Surely it meant something! [5]Does God give you the Spirit and work miracles among you because you do what the Law requires, or because you hear and believe the gospel?

[6]It is just as the scripture says about Abraham, "He believed God, and because of his faith God accepted him as righteous." [7]You should realize, then, that the people who have faith are the real descendants of Abraham. [8]The scripture saw ahead of time that God would put the Gentiles right with himself through faith. And so the scripture preached the Good News to Abraham ahead of time: "Through you God will bless all the people on earth." [9]Abraham believed and was blessed; so all who believe are blessed as he was.

[10]Those who depend on obeying the Law live under a curse. For the scripture says, "Whoever does not always obey everything that is written in the book of the Law is under God's curse!" [11]Now, it is clear that no man is put right with God by means of the Law; because the scripture says, "He who is put right with God through faith shall live." [12]But the Law does not depend on faith. Instead, as the scripture says, "The man who does everything the Law requires will live by it."

[13]But Christ has redeemed us from the curse that the Law brings, by becoming a curse for us; because the scripture says, "Anyone who is hanged on a tree is

under God's curse." ¹⁴Christ did this in order that the blessing God promised Abraham might be given to the Gentiles by means of Christ Jesus, so that we, through faith, might receive the Spirit promised by God.

You are all one in union with Christ Jesus

The Law and the Promise

¹⁵Brothers, I am going to use an everyday example: when two men agree on a matter and sign a covenant, no one can break that covenant or add anything to it. ¹⁶Now, God made his promises to Abraham and to his descendant. The scripture does not say, "and to your descendants," meaning many people. It says, "and to your descendant," meaning one person only, who is Christ. ¹⁷What I mean is this: God made a covenant and promised to keep it. The Law, which came four hundred

and thirty years later, cannot break that covenant and cancel God's promise. [18]For if what God gives depends on the Law, then it no longer depends on his promise. However, it was because God had promised it that he gave it to Abraham.

[19]What was the purpose of the Law, then? It was added in order to show what wrongdoing is, and was meant to last until the coming of Abraham's descendant, to whom the promise was made. The Law was handed down by angels, with a man acting as a go-between. [20]But a go-between is not needed when there is only one person; and God is one.

The Purpose of the Law

[21]Does this mean that the Law is against God's promises? No, not at all! For if a law had been given that could bring life to men, then man could be put right with God through law. [22]But the scripture has said that the whole world is under the power of sin, so that the gift which is promised on the basis of faith in Jesus Christ might be given to those who believe.

[23]Before the time for faith came, however, the Law kept us all locked up as prisoners, until this coming faith should be revealed. [24]So the Law was in charge of us until Christ came, so that we might be put right with God through faith. [25]Now that the time of faith is here, the Law is no longer in charge of us.

[26]It is through faith that all of you are God's sons in union with Christ Jesus. [27]You were baptized into union with Christ, and so have taken upon yourselves the qualities of Christ himself. [28]So there is no difference between Jews and Gentiles, between slaves and free men, between men and women; you are all one in union with Christ Jesus. [29]If you belong to Christ, then you are the descendants of Abraham, and will receive what God has promised.

4   But to continue: the son who will receive his father's property is treated just like a slave while he is young, even though he really owns everything. [2]While he is young, there are men who take care of him and manage his affairs until the time set by his father. [3]In the same way, we too were slaves of the ruling spirits of the universe, before we reached spiritual maturity. [4]But

when the right time finally came, God sent his own Son. He came as the son of a human mother, and lived under the Jewish Law, [5]to redeem those who were under the Law, so that we might become God's sons.

[6]To show that you are his sons, God sent the Spirit of his Son into our hearts, the Spirit who cries, "Father, my Father." [7]So then, you are no longer a slave, but a son. And since you are his son, God will give you all he has for his sons.

You are no longer a slave, but a son

Paul's Concern for the Galatians

[8]In the past you did not know God, and so you were slaves of beings who are not gods. [9]But now that you know God—or, I should say, now that God knows you —how is it that you want to turn back to those weak and pitiful ruling spirits? Why do you want to become their slaves all over again? [10]You pay special attention to certain days, months, seasons, and years. [11]I am afraid for you! Can it be that all my work for you has been for nothing?

[12]I beg you, my brothers, be like me. After all, I am like you. You have not done me any wrong. [13]You remember why I preached the gospel to you the first time; it was because I was sick. [14]But you did not despise

or reject me, even though my physical condition was a great trial to you. Instead, you received me as you would God's angel; you received me as you would Christ Jesus. [15]You were so happy! What has happened? I myself can say this about you: you would have taken out your own eyes, if you could, and given them to me. [16]Have I now become your enemy by telling you the truth?

[17]Those other people show a deep concern for you, but their intentions are not good. All they want is to separate you from me, so that you will have the same concern for them as they have for you. [18]Now, it is good to have such a deep concern for a good purpose —this is true always, and not only when I am with you. [19]My dear children! Once again, just like a mother in childbirth, I feel the same kind of pain for you, until Christ's nature is formed in you. [20]How I wish I were with you now, so that I could take a different attitude towards you. I am so worried about you!

The Example of Hagar and Sarah

[21]Let me ask those of you who want to be subject to the Law: do you not hear what the Law says? [22]It says that Abraham had two sons, one by a slave woman, the other by a free woman. [23]His son by the slave woman was born in the usual way, but his son by the free woman was born as a result of God's promise. [24]This can be taken as a figure: the two women are two covenants, one of which (Hagar, that is) comes from Mount Sinai, whose children are born in slavery. [25]Hagar stands for Mount Sinai in Arabia, and she is a figure of the present city of Jerusalem, a slave with all its people. [26]But the heavenly Jerusalem is free, and she is our mother. [27]For the scripture says,

> "Be happy, woman who never had children!
> Shout and cry with joy, you who never felt the pains of childbirth!
> For the woman who was deserted will have more children
> than the woman living with her husband."

²⁸Now, you, my brothers, are God's children as a result of his promise, just as Isaac was. ²⁹At that time the son who was born in the usual way persecuted the one who was born because of God's Spirit; and it is the same now. ³⁰But what does the scripture say? It says, "Throw out the slave woman and her son; for the son of the slave woman will not share the father's property with the son of the free woman." ³¹So then, my brothers, we are not the children of a slave woman, but of the free woman.

Preserve Your Freedom

5 Freedom is what we have—Christ has set us free! Stand, then, as free men, and do not allow yourselves to become slaves again.

²Listen! I, Paul, tell you this: if you allow yourselves to be circumcised, it means that Christ is of no use to you at all. ³Once more I warn any man who allows himself to be circumcised that he is obliged to obey the whole Law. ⁴Those of you who try to be put right with God by obeying the Law have cut yourselves off from Christ. You are outside God's grace. ⁵As for us, our hope is that God will put us right with him; and this is what we wait for, by the power of God's Spirit working through our faith. ⁶For when we are in union with Christ Jesus, neither circumcision nor the lack of it makes any difference at all; what matters is faith that works through love.

⁷You were doing so well! Who made you stop obeying the truth? How did he persuade you? ⁸It was not done by God, who calls you. ⁹"It takes only a little yeast to raise the whole batch of dough," as they say. ¹⁰But I still feel sure about you. Our union in the Lord makes me confident that you will not take a different view, and that the man who is upsetting you, whoever he is, will be punished by God.

¹¹But as for me, brothers, why am I still persecuted if I continue to preach that circumcision is necessary? If that were true, then my preaching about the cross of Christ would cause no trouble. ¹²I wish that the people who are upsetting you would go all the way; let them go on and castrate themselves!

¹³As for you, my brothers, you were called to be free. But do not let this freedom become an excuse for

letting your physical desires rule you. Instead, let love make you serve one another. [14]For the whole Law is summed up in one commandment: "Love your fellow-man as yourself." [15]But if you act like animals, hurting and harming each other, then watch out, or you will completely destroy one another.

The Spirit and Human Nature

[16]What I say is this: let the Spirit direct your lives, and do not satisfy the desires of the human nature. [17]For what our human nature wants is opposed to what the Spirit wants, and what the Spirit wants is opposed to what human nature wants. The two are enemies, and this means that you cannot do what you want to do. [18]If the Spirit leads you, then you are not subject to the Law.

[19]What human nature does is quite plain. It shows itself in immoral, filthy, and indecent actions; [20]in worship of idols and witchcraft. People become enemies, they fight, become jealous, angry, and ambitious. They separate into parties and groups; [21]they are envious, get drunk, have orgies, and do other things like these. I warn you now as I have before: those who do these things will not receive the Kingdom of God.

[22]But the Spirit produces love, joy, peace, patience, kindness, goodness, faithfulness, [23]humility, and self-control. There is no law against such things as these. [24]And those who belong to Christ Jesus have put to death their human nature, with all its passions and desires. [25]The Spirit has given us life; he must also control our lives. [26]We must not be proud, or irritate one another, or be jealous of one another.

Bear One Another's Burdens

6 My brothers, if someone is caught in any kind of wrongdoing, those of you who are spiritual should set him right; but you must do it in a gentle way. And keep an eye on yourself, so that you will not be tempted, too. [2]Help carry one another's burdens, and in this way you will obey the law of Christ. [3]If someone thinks he is something, when he really is nothing, he is only fooling himself. [4]Each one should judge his own conduct for

himself. If it is good, then he can be proud of what he himself has done, without having to compare it with what someone else has done. ⁵For everyone has to carry his own load.

⁶The man who is being taught the Christian message should share all the good things he has with his teacher.

⁷Do not deceive yourselves; no one makes a fool of God. A man will reap exactly what he plants. ⁸If he plants in the field of his natural desires, from it he will gather the harvest of death; if he plants in the field of the Spirit, from the Spirit he will gather the harvest of eter-

Do good to everyone

nal life. ⁹So let us not become tired of doing good; for if we do not give up, the time will come when we will reap the harvest. ¹⁰So then, as often as we have the chance, we should do good to everyone, but especially to those who belong to our family in the faith.

Final Warning and Greeting

¹¹See what big letters I make as I write to you now with my own hand! ¹²Those who want to show off and brag about external matters are the ones who are trying to force you to be circumcised. They do it, however, only that they may not be persecuted for the cross of Christ. ¹³Even those who practise circumcision do not obey the Law; they want you to be circumcised so they can boast that you submitted to this physical ceremony. ¹⁴As for me, however, I will boast only of the cross of our Lord Jesus Christ; for by means of his cross the

world is dead to me, and I am dead to the world. [15]It does not matter at all whether or not one is circumcised. What does matter is being a new creature. [16]As for those who follow this rule in their lives, may peace and mercy be with them—with them and with all God's people!

[17]To conclude: let no one give me any more trouble, because the scars I have on my body show that I am the slave of Jesus.

[18]May the grace of our Lord Jesus Christ be with you all, my brothers. Amen.

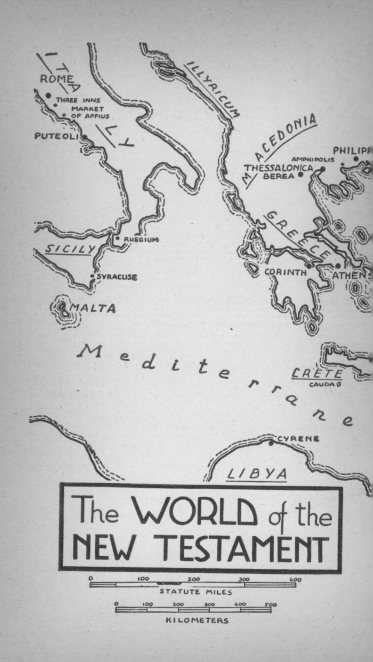

The WORLD of the NEW TESTAMENT

THE BIBLE READING FELLOWSHIP

Readers of this commentary may wish to follow a regular pattern of Bible reading, designed to cover the Bible roughly on the basis of a book a month. Suitable Notes (send for details) with helpful exposition and prayers are provided by the Bible Reading Fellowship three times a year (January to April, May to August, September to December), and are available from:—

UK   The Bible Reading Fellowship,
St Michael's House,
2 Elizabeth Street,
London, SW1W 9RQ

USA   The Bible Reading Fellowship,
P.O. Box 299, Winter Park,
Florida 32789, USA.

AUSTRALIA The Bible Reading Fellowship,
Jamieson House,
Constitution Avenue, Reid,
Canberra, ACT 2601,
Australia.

Good News for Modern Man

The New Testament: Today's English Version

'I commend this version . . . an outstanding addition to the Fontana Religious Series.'
Archbishop of York

'TEV with its scrupulous accuracy and fresh contemporary language makes a valuable contribution to a better understanding of God's revealed Word. It will be helpful in particular to all those who are engaged in the pursuit of the two principal ecumenical aims of twentieth-century Christianity: renewal and reunion. I am grateful to Collins Publishers for including TEV in its Religious Fontana Series and wish it every best success.'
Archbishop H. E. Cardinale, Apostolic Delegate to Great Britain

'As new as the new year the British paperback edition of the New Testament Today's English Version GOOD NEWS FOR MODERN MAN will in the coming weeks be catching the public eye on bookshop counters, at street-corner, railway and airport bookstalls, in tobacconists, general stores, and supermarkets. The Good News will be where the people go.'
Methodist Recorder

Good News for Modern Man

Editions available in the United Kingdom published by Collins Fontana Books

Sing a New Song
  (The Psalms in Today's English Version)   20p

Good News for Modern Man
  (The New Testament in Today's English Version)

  3rd edition   40p
  Available in hardback   65p

Published jointly by the British and Foreign Bible Society and the National Bible Society of Scotland in association with Collins Fontana Books.

New Testament illustrated paperback   35p

New Testament paperback without illustrations   25p

Single books with illustrations
  Matthew   80 pages   6p
  Mark   64 pages   6p
  Luke   84 pages   5p
  John   64 pages   5p
  Philippians   16 pages   4p
Each Gospel available in large type   20p

Also available in the Fontana Religious Series

Good News in Luke
WILF WILKINSON

Luke's gospel is probably the most loved part of the whole New Testament – with many famous stories, some by Jesus, some by Luke himself, full of the joy and compassion of the Good News. Here it is introduced by a Church of England vicar who is a well known broadcaster, with an artist's eye and a human touch.

Good News in John
DOUGLAS WEBSTER

John's gospel is for many people the most marvellous piece of writing in existence. Certainly there is nothing else like it – which is one of the reasons why it needs explaining. Here it is introduced by Canon Douglas Webster of St Paul's Cathedral, well known for his teaching of the Bible in many countries.

Good News in Acts
DAVID EDWARDS

The Acts of the Apostles tells the story of how Christianity spread from Jerusalem to Rome. Here, breaking away from any sacred geography about the journeys of St Paul, the excitement and meaning of the drama are conveyed by Canon David Edwards of Westminster Abbey.

Good News in Romans
JOSEPH RHYMER

Paul's letter to the Romans is a personal message from an intelligent, sensitive and very experienced man, spelling out the Christian faith as he understands it. Here its meaning is explained by a Roman Catholic teacher of the Bible, Joseph Rhymer. Then Paul's message about human life is related to four modern plays or novels by another scholar, Joseph Griffiths.